FOR LIFE

T0324343

FOR LIFE

DEFENDING THE DEFENSELESS

JOHN BORNSCHEIN

With a special section by
Rob Schwarzwalder and Cathy Cleaver Ruse
of the Family Research Council

KIRKDALE PRESS

For Life: Defending the Defenseless

Copyright 2014 John Bornschein

Kirkdale Press, 1313 Commercial St., Bellingham, WA 98225
KirkdalePress.com

All rights reserved. You may use brief quotations from this book in reviews, presentations, articles, and books. For all other uses, please write Kirkdale Press for permission. Email us at permissions@kirkdalepress.com.

Unless otherwise indicated, all Scripture quotations are taken from the Holy Bible, New International Version, NIV. Copyright 1973, 1978, 1984, 2011 by Biblica, Inc. All rights reserved worldwide. www.zondervan.com.

ISBN: 978-1-57799-544-9

Cover Design: Christine Gerhart
Typesetting: projectluz.com

CONTENTS

INTRODUCTION

For Life—what does the title of this book *really* mean? The answer is simple. This book was written to encourage and inspire you to stand boldly on the front lines of our culture today in defense of the defenseless—possibly the greatest cause in the modern era, second only to the declaration and commission of evangelism. Indeed, throughout these pages you will find a tapestry woven with the fibers of life and revelation. I believe the four key points I've presented in this book will challenge you to commit yourself to the preservation of life at all stages.

Christ challenged us to grab the plow and never look back (Luke 9:62). You will soon find yourself at a crossroad where the path less traveled awaits, but where the indescribable blessings of eternity abound. I am prayerfully optimistic that once you embark on this journey of truth, you will have a transformation of the mind that will lead you into a life-long service—one that is not for the faint of heart. You will encounter some surprises along the way, including very real and personal stories of redemption and hope. But such is life when we watch the hand of God move in and through people.

On January 22, 1973, the U.S. Supreme Court struck down every state anti-abortion law through two rulings: *Roe v. Wade* and *Doe v. Bolton*. Since then, 55 million babies have been aborted in the United States alone.[1] According to many pregnancy-center studies and Focus on the Family, about one in three women will have an abortion by age 45.[2] Forty-four percent of women who had abortions in the U.S. had at least one previous abortion.[3] Eighty-two percent of women who had abortions in the U.S. were unmarried,[4] and 50 percent of U.S. women having abortions are younger than 25.[5] All of this has led to 1.37 million babies being aborted in America every year—almost 4,000 babies per day.[6]

The book you are about to read is a message from the heart. Lives are being impacted—even lost—as you read these words. There is no time to lose. Let's get started.

1. "An Overview of Abortion in the United States," Guttmacher Institute, numbers updated as of January 22, 2013, http://www.guttmacher.org/media/presskits/2005/06/28/abortionoverview.html.

2. "Facts on Induced Abortion in the United Sates," Guttmacher Institute, July 2008, accessed August 13, 2008, http://www.guttmacher.org/pubs/fb_induced_abortion.html.

3. "Abortion Surveillance 2004 Report," Center for Disease Control and Prevention, November 23, 2007, accessed August 13, 2008, http://www.cdc.gov/mmwr/PDF/ss/ss5609.pdf.

4. "Abortion Surveillance 2004 Report," Center for Disease Control and Prevention, November 23, 2007, accessed August 13, 2008, http://www.cdc.gov/mmwr/PDF/ss/ss5609.pdf.

5. "Facts on Induced Abortion in the United Sates," Guttmacher Institute, July 2008, accessed August 13, 2008, http://www.guttmacher.org/pubs/fb_induced_abortion.html.

6. "Abortion Statistics: United States Data and Trends," National Right to Life, accessed November 1, 2007, http://www.nrlc.org/abortion/facts/abortionstats.html.

SEE IT

The Splendor of an Awesome God

I was born into some pretty rough circumstances. It's only by the grace of God that I am able to write these words to you now. In fact, in chapter three, I will share with you a bit of my own journey.

Because of God, a lowly man like me has been blessed with an incredible family, an amazing wife, and five beautiful children who know and love the Lord. But it wasn't always this way. I am in awe and humbled each and every day that God uses the lowly things of this world to bring down the strong—even the foolish to shame the wise (1 Cor 1:27).

That is my résumé. I like things simple. God gives it to me simple, so I am going to share with you in a simple manner. But don't take it personally—that is just how I am wired.

Establishing a Baseline

I once sat on a plane next to a campaign manager who was working with a prominent politician. After he glanced over and noticed my reading material, he made a comment that was a bit derogatory. Without allowing me to first share my foundational principles, he acted on his perceptions and attempted to challenge the perspectives he assumed I had. Once I was able to point him to 2 Timothy 3:16, where Paul says that all Scripture is God-breathed and infallible, there were no further misconceptions of what I believed and why. He didn't necessarily agree with my viewpoint, but I dropped some seeds of truth on his desert floor that were ripe for the waters of heaven. To this day, I still pray for him.

It was pointless for us to debate issues without getting to the root of our cause. He was trying to change my outward focus on a particular subject matter, all the while completely skirting the obvious questions that were necessary for a fruitful and productive conversation. In order to engage in a fruitful discussion, we needed to first establish a baseline.

That's the purpose of this chapter: to establish a baseline for the rest of the book. If we don't have a good baseline to understand each other, then the rest of this material won't align correctly. First, let's talk about God.

Let's face it—God is a big God, and we are privileged to behold even a fraction of His majesty. That is a fact. We constantly take His presence for granted, yet all around us the rocks cry out in praise to His holy name. If you don't believe me, stop and listen. In the Bible, God says, "Be still, and know that I am God" (Psa 46:10). These powerful words should frame what I am about to say next.

The Bible is very clear about the fact that God exists and that He created the whole world and all that is in it. This is *fact*—not fiction, not myth. As Anthony DeStefano states so well in his book *Ten Prayers God Always Says Yes To,*

There isn't much room for compromise here. Either we're alone in the world or we're not. Either we came about by chance or we were created for a reason. Either death is the end or it's the beginning. Either our situation is ultimately hopeless or it's ultimately blissful. There really can't be two more different or diametrically opposed worldviews. So how can we come to grips with this most profound question? Some of the greatest geniuses the world has ever known—Aristotle, Plato, Augustine, Aquinas, Spinoza, Pascal, Descartes and Kant, to name a few— have made the case that there is a God, and that He is a real, living being. In the case of faith, it's easy to overlook the most fundamental point of all, namely, that God is not an argument; He is not a syllogism; He is not even a concept. God is a living being. He has the ability to know things, to desire things, to create things, and to love things. He is fully aware and involved. He is alive.[1]

Theology is our understanding of God. The term literally means "*logos* about *Theos*" or "a word about God." The Christian faith is built on the foundation of trust in an Almighty God who has revealed Himself to humanity. God the Father is the one who created the universe and sustains it, all while desiring a relationship with each one of us. "Almighty" means that God is sovereign over His creation. With wisdom and love, and in power and control, God presides over all things. His sovereignty

---

1. Anthony DeStefano, *Ten Prayers God Always Says Yes To* (New York: Doubleday, 2007), 10–11.

is a source of comfort and truth for believers. We know that nothing happens without His knowledge and permission.

The words "creator of heaven and earth" reflect our belief that all things were created by an orderly, wise God. Life has meaning and purpose. Humans bear God's image and likeness; therefore, all of life is to be respected, and creation should be valued. The complexity and design of the world around us leads us to the conclusion that there must be a grand designer or creator. Empirical evidence found in life, chemistry, astrobiology, and physics suggests purpose, design, order, and meaning. Psalm 19:1 tells us that the created world points to the God who is its infinite, originating source: "The heavens declare [or "bear witness to"] the glory of God; the skies [or "expanse"] proclaim the work of his hands."

What separates God from the rest of the spiritual or unseen entities—or even that which is in the physical world—is the fact that He is the *only* source of creation and life. There is no tangible evidence that suggests otherwise. The only God, who goes by many names—God, Yahweh, the Alpha and the Omega—created the vast expanse of the universe and all that is within it, along with all dimensions, space, time, and the beings that inhabit them. And He created all of this from absolutely nothing.

We cannot look at the universe without seeing intelligent design. Human beings have never created something from nothing. We have manipulated and shaped elements and worked within the confines of natural laws, but we have never created something from nothing. Even the theory of evolution is based on the "change in the inherited traits of a population of organisms through successive generations."[2] It is the theory of natural selection over a large span of time. Regardless of the amount of time that is required for evolution to take place, the theory self-destructs when origin is examined. There is no beginning to the process that has a viable source without a creator. Thus, we are right back to confronting the fact that an intelligent designer is at work, an engineer of a very complex system.

R.C. Sproul writes, "Men are never duly touched and impressed with a conviction of their insignificance, until they have contrasted themselves with the majesty of God."[3] I am constantly astounded when I look to the heavens. Aren't you? I have made my home in Colorado where, on the perfect night, you can sit outside, roll out a blanket, put your head back, and be left speechless by what your eyes behold. It is overwhelming to witness the grand creativity of our awesome God.

When I view these sights, I am drawn right to Scriptures where we are told, "By the word of the LORD the heavens were made, their starry host by the breath of his mouth" (Psa 33:6). In Isaiah 48:13 God tells us, "My own hand laid the foundations of the earth, and my right hand spread out the heavens; when I summon them, they all stand up together." An earlier passage in Isaiah declares,

> "To whom will you compare me? Or who is my equal?" says the Holy One. Lift up your eyes and look to the heavens: Who created all these? He who brings out the starry host one by one and calls forth each of

2. A. A. Forbes and B. A. Krimmel, "Evolution Is Change in the Inherited Traits of a Population through Successive Generations," *Nature Education Knowledge*, 2010, http://www.nature.com/scitable/knowledge/library/evolution-is-change-in-the-inherited-traits-15164254.

3. R.C. Sproul, *The Holiness of God* (Wheaton, IL: Tyndale, 1985), 72.

> them by name. Because of his great power and mighty
> strength, not one of them is missing. ... Do you not
> know? Have you not heard? The Lord is the everlasting
> God, the Creator of the ends of the earth. He will not
> grow tired or weary, and His understanding no one
> can fathom (Isaiah 40:25–26, 28).

In the New Testament, Paul attests to Jesus' role in creation
when he writes, "The Son is the image of the invisible God, the
firstborn over all creation. For in him all things were created:
things in heaven and on earth, visible and invisible, whether
thrones or powers or rulers or authorities; all things have been
created through him and for him" (Col 1:15–16). I also encourage
you to read Psalm 8:1–4 and Isaiah 40:12. I trust you see where I
am going with all of this?

Perspective

Let's look at the science. Stars, other than our sun, are so far
distant that astronomers refer to their distances not in terms of
kilometers or miles, but in light years. Light is the fastest moving
stuff in the universe. It travels at an incredible 186,000 miles
(300,000 kilometers) per second. If you could travel at the speed
of light, you would be able to circle the earth's equator about 7.5
times in just one second.

Okay, now stay with me. A light year is the distance light
travels in one year. How far is that? Multiply the number of
seconds in one year by the number of miles (or kilometers) that
light travels in one second, and there you have it: one light year.
Let me help you with the math. We are talking 5.88 trillion miles
(9.5 trillion kilometers).

Let's put that into perspective. The Milky Way is a huge
city of stars, so big that even at the speed of light, it would take

100,000 years to travel across it. If you were to pull a quarter out of your pocket right now and toss it on the ground, then look at the world around it, the quarter starts to look pretty small. Well, our solar system is the size of a quarter in the entire North American continent by comparison—and that is just our Milky Way galaxy. There are billions of galaxies that are even bigger than ours.

Hold up your hand and look at the amount of space between your thumb and pinky fingers. I hope you notice the many intricacies of your hand. Quite amazing, isn't it? Think about what can be accomplished with just the opposable thumb. But aside from that, you probably noticed the few inches of open space between those fingers. In the Bible, it says that God holds the Pleiades in His hand (Job 38:31–33; Amos 5:8). The Pleiades is a cluster of seven stars. The radius is about eight light years, and the tidal radius is about 43 light years across. That means you would be traveling 186,000 miles per second for 43 years. Yet God holds that entire span in His hand.

Don't you see? The universe declares His wonder. There are so many stars in just the Milky Way galaxy that it would take you 2,500 years to count every one if you counted one every second.

Now, imagine this: Dr. Michael Behe, a biophysics professor at Lehigh University, argues that the human body is more complex than the earth and its entire ecological system—perhaps even more complex than the universe itself. How amazing is that? There are over 3 billion DNA codes in the human body. The same proteins that make up the human brain also make up the liver. It is the DNA coding that aligns them to form the right organ. This language is more complex than any signal studied in space, and it is right under our nose—literally.

When you look up, you see the splendor of His work, and when you look down, you see the splendor of His work. You are surrounded by it, and it is all beautiful and designed by a creator for a purpose. That means you were created for a purpose. God does not waste His time or talents. With the same level of detail and perfection that He created the heavens above, He created you. King David wrote in the book of Psalms:

> I praise you because I am fearfully and wonderfully made; your works are wonderful, I know that full well. My frame was not hidden from you when I was made in the secret place, when I was woven together in the depths of the earth. Your eyes saw my unformed body; all the days ordained for me were written in your book before one of them came to be (Psa 139:14–16).

We have a God of details—an orderly and wise God who assembles for purpose. Amazingly, He knows the number of hairs on your head (Matt 10:30). Your fingerprints, your eyes, your wrinkles (I have a few more of those these days), even your hair color—all of these are unique. There are 7 billion people walking the earth and billions more who have gone before them, yet no two humans are alike. We are all individually designed by a God who loves life.

Listen to what God says here: "Before I formed you in the womb I knew you, before you were born I set you apart" (Jer 1:5). Before you were born, God knew you. That means the artist was working on His masterpiece, shaping the clay vessel while it was cooking in the oven. When you were born, you were perfect in design—freckles, wrinkles, and all.

I am so glad your mother chose life—aren't you? You are a living, breathing masterpiece, and the Father looks down with pleasure at the work of His hands. We only need to realize this to make His heart beat with joy. It is a day of rejoicing when the creation recognizes the creator and their contribution to the canvas of life.

A God Who Loves Life

We have a God who loves life. He loves life so much that He gave His own life to preserve it—to save it, even from itself. If you are seeking Him, I will be in prayer for you as you embark on the greatest, most important journey of your life. There are eternal consequences, but I know God will reveal Himself as long as you remain steadfast in your pursuit. In Scripture Christ declares, "Here I am! I stand at the door and knock. If anyone hears my voice and opens the door, I will come in and eat with that person, and they with me" (Rev 3:20).

Without Christ, we only get half the story. The whole plan of God unfolds before our eyes from cover to cover of the canonized Scriptures. It is truly a beautiful story of hope and the redemption of humankind by a gracious and holy God who loves us so much that He takes the full blunt of our punishment. According to Scripture, "There is no one righteous, not even one" (Rom 3:10). Thus, we know that it truly is "by grace you have been saved, through faith—and this is not from yourselves, it is the gift of God" (Eph 2:8). We did not earn this amazing gift of hope and life. Just as Jesus tells us in John 14:6, "I am the way and the truth and the life. No one comes to the Father except through me."

I have looked at the religions of the world, and either there is a vague understanding of who "god" is—driven purely by emotion or a state of mind—or there are angry "god or gods" who leave little hope for anyone. In this case, only your actions will determine if you are worthy—you must perform, and then maybe you have a chance. Only Jesus Christ offers real hope, love, compassion, and personal relationship. Other "gods" are sculpted and defined by people.

The beauty and revealed mysteries of Scripture are beyond human comprehension. In his book *Who Is This Man?* John Ortberg writes of Jesus' widespread impact on all aspects of culture, from the way people view children, to the education system, compassion, humility, forgiveness, and humanitarian reform. He quotes Yale historian Jeroslav Pelikan, who wrote,

> Regardless of what anyone may personally think or believe about him, Jesus of Nazareth has been the dominant figure in the history of Western Culture for almost 20 centuries. If it were possible, with some sort of super magnet, to pull up out of history every scrap of metal bearing at least a trace of his name, how much would be left?[4]

Ortberg declares, "It turns out that the life of Jesus is a comet with an exceedingly long tale. … The unpredictable influence of that carpenter continues to endure and spread across the world."[5] Jeremiah 29:13 reminds us, "You will seek me and find me when you seek me with all your heart." Remember these powerful words and you will always *see it*: "Ask and it will be given to you; seek and you will find; knock and the door will be opened to you" (Matt 7:7).

---

4. Jaroslav Pelikan, *Jesus Through the Centuries: His Place in the History of Culture* (New Haven: Yale University Press, 1985), 1.

5. John Ortberg, *Who Is This Man? The Unpredictable Impact of the Inescapable Jesus* (Grand Rapids, MI: Zondervan, 2012). See also Ortberg, "Six Surprising Ways Jesus Changed the World," *Huffington Post,* August 13, 2012, http://www.huffingtonpost.com/john-ortberg/six-surprising-ways-jesus-b_1773225.html.

KNOW IT

The Accountability
We Have before Him

I have some news for you that is beyond comprehension. Are you ready for it? You were created in the image of God. That is mind blowing when you think about it. Genesis 1:27 observes, "So God created mankind in his own image, in the image of God he created them; male and female he created them." What does that mean exactly? Let's look at what some noted theologians have to say on the matter.[1]

Thomas Aquinas identified the image of God as "the human ability to think and reason, to use language and art, far surpassing the abilities of any animals."[2] In Leonard Verduin's view, the image of God "consists in our dominion over animals and plants,

---

1. Special thanks to Phil Williams, historian and researcher.

2. Thomas Aquinas, "Man to the Image of God," cited in Millard J. Erickson, ed., *Readings in Christian Theology, Volume 2: Man's Need and God's Gift* (Grand Rapids, MI: Baker Publishing Group, 1976), 37–43; "Humans in the Image of God," Grace Communion International, accessed October 7, 2010, http://www.gci.org/humans/image.

which continues despite our sinfulness."[3] G.W. Bromiley notes that "A 'widely accepted interpretation' is that the 'image' is our ability to make moral decisions, which involve self-awareness and social awareness."[4] According to Emil Brunner, the image is "our ability to have a relationship with God, reflected in the tendency of all societies to have forms of worship."[5]

Elements of the *Imago Dei*

Many theologians believe there are three common elements within the concept of *imago Dei* (the "image of God"): substantive, relational, and functional. Let's explore each of these elements further.

Substantive

The substantive element refers to the idea that humans were formed in the likeness of God in both characteristics and physical form. Many believe that God crafted our very design from His own makeup. According to this theory, God inhabits a body, and He used this perfect, flawless vessel as a blueprint for the human structure.

In addition, we are formed in His likeness by our characteristics—our free will. We are not programmed by

---

3. Leonard Verduin, "A Dominion-Haver," cited in Erickson, *Readings in Christian Theology*, 55–74; "Humans in the Image of God," Grace Communion.

4. G.W. Bromiley, "Image of God," cited in G.W. Bromiley, ed., *International Standard Bible Encyclopedia, vol. 2* (Grand Rapids, MI: Eerdmans, 1988), 804; "Humans in the Image of God," Grace Communion.

5. Emil Brunner, "Man and Creation," cited in Erickson, *Readings in Christian Theology*, 45–54; "Humans in the Image of God," Grace Communion.

instinct, design, or function. We can execute decisions based on our thoughts. Martin Luther suggested that humanity possessed the character of holiness—morality and love for God.

Relational

The relational element is based on the theology that we had a relationship with God before the fall of humanity, and to retain the image of God, we must have the Holy Spirit dwelling within us through a relationship with Christ. It is this gift that separates us from other complex living creatures. We are not organic machines. Rather, we are living souls who have a destination in the spiritual realm. We are symbiotic creations, evidenced by the fact that our living, breathing, physical body is controlled by a living soul.

Functional

The functional element focuses more on the second part of Genesis 1:26, which states, "Let us make mankind in our image … so that they may rule over the fish of the sea and the birds of the air, over the livestock and all the wild animals, and over all the creatures that move along the ground." This theory suggests that the authority over creation is the image of God. God has authority over all creation, but He has granted this authority to humankind over the earth. Thus, all creation on earth is subject to the rule of humankind, just as the universe is subject to God.

The Artist's Eye

Let's review a few verses I pointed out in chapter one. In Psalm 139:14–16, the psalmist praises God, declaring,

> I praise you because I am fearfully and wonderfully made; your works are wonderful, I know that full well. My frame was not hidden from you when I was made in the secret place, when I was woven together in the depths of the earth. Your eyes saw my unformed body; all the days ordained for me were written in your book before one of them came to be.

God tells the prophet Jeremiah something similar in Jeremiah 1:5: "Before I formed you in the womb I knew you, before you were born I set you apart." Here is another, similar verse that we often overlook: "This is what the LORD says—he who made you, who formed you in the womb, and who will help you: Do not be afraid … my servant … whom I have chosen" (Isa 44:2). In each of these passages, we see a common thread: God knew the person before He made the body. Thus, each life is precious and made perfectly by His hand, in His image.

No child is an accident. Our God is creative, providing characteristics, shapes, colors, and abilities to all, making each person wonderfully unique. Just because someone is different doesn't make them a flawed design. An autistic child is blessed. The blind, the deaf, and the mute are blessed and perfect in the Grand Artist's eyes. Each person experiences life differently, and all are equal contributors in His story.

Some of God's most unique creations have done more than many of us ever will. Joni Eareckson Tada, a paraplegic and a dear friend of mine, has blessed millions of people with her teaching ministry. Nick Vujicic, born with no legs or arms, has brought tens of thousands of people to the Lord through his message of hope. My legacy will pale in comparison to what God is doing through them, and they are an inspiration to us all—to God be the glory.

Since you, too, are formed in the image of God, you are perfectly equipped to do His work. Therefore, no one should ever be denied the opportunity to live out their life in accordance to His will. There are no boundaries when we reside in the hands of an almighty God. In the words of the Apostle Paul, "What, then, shall we say in response to these things? If God is for us, who can be against us?" (Rom 8:31).

A Divided Nation

Let's look back at the 2012 U.S. presidential elections for a moment and examine the state of our nation. Over a period of 18 months, our nation spent more than 5.8 billion dollars to influence Americans to not only exercise their right to vote, but to vote for the leaders who identified with their perspectives. After spending a staggering $49.50 to drive each of the 117 million votes (at the time of decision), the nation was split almost 50/50 on the primaries—with less than two percent separating the candidates. Despite a hard-fought campaign by both sides, the leadership of this nation remained virtually unchanged in every branch of government, despite four years of unprecedented, compounding challenges affecting every area of our society. In the aftermath of the 2012 elections—and the most expensive social survey ever conducted—we were left only with the reminder that America is a divided nation.

Abraham Lincoln, quoting from Mark 3:24, boldly stated that "a house divided against itself cannot stand." The issues that divided our nation during the 2012 elections were of greater significance than the prevailing economic scrutiny. The moral values of the sanctity of human life, preservation of marriage, defense of Israel, and religious freedoms became the overwhelming subject of many attack ads, speeches, and debates.

There seemed to be more emphasis on the definition of marriage and the defense of the unborn than ever before.

Candidates aligned with opposing sides of the spectrum, leaving no middle ground. Based on the arguments, life was described as either (1) sacred and meant to be preserved, no matter the circumstances, or (2) a decision—not a right. Marriage was described as between one man and one woman, as it was from the beginning, or it was left to interpretation and redefinition based on social moral relativism.

We must examine ourselves as a nation. Aside from party affiliation, the election was clearly a revelation of the voter's values. The problem isn't as much the politicians in Washington D.C. as we would like to believe. The problem is in our homes, our communities, and even our churches. Indeed, the heart of the American people has changed.

How far have we digressed as a nation? In 1620, William Bradford and the brave men and women of faith aboard the Mayflower declared America to be "for the glory of God and the advancement of the Christian faith." Later it was President George Washington who said that the twin pillars essential for supporting a successful society are morality and religion. What kind of religion? Was it just any kind? John Adams, our second president, clarified this when he declared, "The general principles on which the fathers achieved independence were … the general principles of Christianity."

Where are we today? Stephen Hopewell describes our current state of affairs:

> The pillar of traditional morality is certainly one that needs to be restored to our society; but we will have to separate it once and for all from the other pillar, that of progress. It is no longer possible for us to see

America as 'the leader in moral progress,' a conceit which has made us blind to the real moral decline in our society and susceptible to believing that our supposed moral goodness can serve to defend us from enemies and invaders.[6]

Are we still a Christian nation? For those of us who align with this faith, the easy answer is yes—but the reality is more difficult to process. According to recent surveys, including one from the Pew Forum on Religion and Public Life, the fastest growing "religious" group in America is made up of people with no religion at all. This group has grown by 25 percent in the past five years, and for the first time evangelicals and Protestants now make up only 48 percent of the population. There was a significant decline in the group who identified themselves as Christian—by as much as 14 percent since 2005.[7]

This alarming trend provides a pathway to power for individuals whose perspectives do not align with those of our Founding Fathers or the general precepts of morality we have strived to preserve for 393 years.[8] Proverbs 29:2 reminds us, "When the righteous are in authority, the people rejoice; but when the wicked rule, the people groan" (NRSV). Noah Webster, a Founding Father and educator, offered a similar warning:

Let it be impressed on your mind that God commands you to choose for rulers just men who will rule in the fear of God (Exod 18:21). ... If the citizens neglect

6. Stephen Hopewell, "The Three Pillars of American Civilization," *The Heritage American* (blog), December 22, 2008, http://heritageamerican.wordpress.com/2008/12/22/the-three-pillars-of-american-civilization/.
7. "'Nones' on the Rise," The Pew Forum on Religion & Public Life, October 9, 2012, http://www.pewforum.org/Unaffiliated/nones-on-the-rise.aspx.
8. That is, since the Mayflower Compact

> their duty and place unprincipled men in office, the
> government will so be corrupted ... If government
> fails to secure public prosperity and happiness, it must
> be because the citizens neglect the Divine commands,
> and elect bad men to make and administer the laws.[9]

We have no one to blame but ourselves. We have failed to pass a legacy of faith to the next generation as God Himself directed us to do (Deut 6:1–9; Psa 78). In four generations, we have lost a firm foundation on moral truth. Now the heart of our nation is divided, and we must be reminded of what the prophets spoke to the people of Israel—a reminder that is still relevant to us today: If we repent and return to God, He will hear, forgive, and restore our land (2 Chr 7:14). It was the Lord who said to Isaiah, "their hearts are far from me" (Isa 29:13). Again He spoke to Jeremiah and said that if His wayward people would return to Him with all their hearts, then He would give them leaders who honor Him—"shepherds after [His] own heart" (Jer 3:6–18). You see, it begins with us assuming a humble, contrite spirit before our Almighty God, expecting nothing in return.

God knows what He's doing—a fact that we, His people, need to be reminded of. This was true of Job, who stated, "Surely I spoke of things I did not understand, things too wonderful for me to know" (Job 42:3). Max Lucado challenged me with these words:

> It's easy to thank God when he does what we want.
> But God doesn't always do what we want. Ask Job.
> His empire collapsed, his children were killed, and
> what was a healthy body became a rage of boils. From

---

9. Noah Webster, *Noah Webster's Advice to the Young and Moral Catechism* (Aledo, TX: WallBuilders, 1993), 36.

whence came this torrent? From whence will come any help? Job goes straight to God and pleads his case. His head hurts. His body hurts. His heart hurts. And God answers. Not with answers but with questions. An ocean of questions. After several dozen questions, Job gets the point. What is it? The point is this: God owes no one anything. No reasons. No explanations. Nothing. If He gave them, we couldn't understand them. God is God. He knows what He is doing. When you can't trace His hand, trust His heart.[10]

God says that He saw the end from the beginning (Isa 46:10), that He is omnipresent (Psa 139:1–18), and that there are no accidents, for all things are according to the counsel of His will (Eph 1:11). Do we believe it? Even when tragedy strikes or we experience a refining defeat, He already has the victory and assures us of such. King David recognized God's sovereignty and sang Him praise: "Yours, LORD, is the greatness and the power and the glory and the majesty and the splendor, for everything in heaven and earth is yours. Yours, LORD, is the kingdom; you are exalted as head over all. Wealth and honor come from you; you are the ruler of all things. In your hands are strength and power to exalt and give strength to all" (1 Chr 29:11–12). Scripture declares that God directs the hearts of the rulers of the earth and selects them for His bidding (Prov 21:1; 8:15; Dan 4:25; Col 1:15–20). The battle is not lost—God is still hearing the cries of His people.

Prayer is needed in America to restore the foundations of Christianity in our homes. Now is not the time to grow weary.

---

10. Max Lucado and Terri A. Gibbs, *God's Inspirational Promises* (Nashville, TN: J. Countryman, 2001), 161.

Now is not the time to give up. God has identified for us the chinks in our armor and the hindering sins that prevail within, so that we gird up our loins and prepare in solemn assembly as never before. We must not allow our prayers to diminish. Rather, we must amplify our prayers with persistence and perseverance. In the words of the Apostle Paul, "Thanks be to God! He gives us the victory through our Lord Jesus Christ. Therefore, my dear brothers and sisters, stand firm. Let nothing move you. Always give yourselves fully to the work of the Lord, because you know that your labor in the Lord is not in vain" (1 Cor 15:56). May our days be filled with praise and adoration for the King of kings. Let our faith be contagious with our passion of service, and may the joy of our love for Him fill our home and impact generations not yet born. We must be intentional for such a time as this.

Under God

Groups like Planned Parenthood and the Freedom From Religion Foundation, among others, oppose the idea that people are accountable to an Almighty God. But this is "nothing new under the sun," as the author of Ecclesiastes once said (Eccl 1:9). Generation after generation, people seek to tear down the institutions that uphold what remaining moral layers prevail within a civilized society, offering nothing in return. After all, it is easier to tear down than to build up.

Consider this letter from Benjamin Franklin to Thomas Paine in response to Paine's controversial book, *Age of Reason*:

> I have read your manuscript with some attention. By the argument it contains against a particular Providence, though you allow a general Providence, you strike at the foundations of all religion. For without the belief of a Providence, that takes cognizance of, guards, and

guides, and may favor particular persons, there is no motive to worship a Deity, to fear his displeasure, or to pray for his protection. I will not enter into any discussion of your principles, though you seem to desire it. At present I shall only give you my opinion, that, though your reasonings are subtle and may prevail with some readers, you will not succeed so as to change the general sentiments of mankind on that subject, and the consequence of printing this piece will be, a great deal of odium drawn upon yourself, mischief to you, and no benefit to others. He that spits against the wind, spits in his own face.

But, were you to succeed, do you imagine any good would be done by it? You yourself may find it easy to live a virtuous life, without the assistance afforded by religion; you having a clear perception of the advantages of virtue, and the disadvantages of vice, and possessing a strength of resolution sufficient to enable you to resist common temptations. But think how great a portion of mankind consists of weak and ignorant men and women, and of inexperienced, inconsiderate youth of both sexes, who have need of the motives of religion to restrain them from vice, to support their virtue, and retain them in the practice of it till it becomes habitual, which is the great point for its security. And perhaps you are indebted to her originally, that is, to your religious education, for the habits of virtue upon which you now justly value yourself. You might easily display your excellent talents of reasoning upon a less hazardous subject, and thereby obtain a rank with our most distinguished authors. For among us it is not necessary, as among the Hottentots, that a youth, to be raised into the company of men, should prove his manhood by beating his mother.

I would advise you, therefore, not to attempt unchaining the tiger, but to burn this piece before it is seen by any other person; whereby you will save yourself a great deal of mortification by the enemies it may raise against you, and perhaps a good deal of regret and repentance. If men are so wicked with religion, what would they be if without it. I intend this letter itself as a proof of my friendship, and therefore add no professions to it.[11]

Despite Franklin's objections, Paine published his *Age of Reason*, infuriating many of the Founding Fathers. John Adams wrote, "The Christian religion is, above all the religions that ever prevailed or existed in ancient or modern times, the religion of wisdom, virtue, equity and humanity, let the Blackguard [meaning "scoundrel," "rogue"] Paine say what he will."[12] The idea of a people being united as *one nation under God* is like nails on a chalkboard to those who seek to run the streets of America with the fruit that brought Eden to ruin.

We cannot ignore the irony regarding those who seek to argue the case for atheism when they state that they have the truth to open the minds of people. The fact remains that it was God Himself who came to liberate the minds of men; He stated this clearly in the Gospel of John: "Then you will know the truth, and the truth will set you free" (John 8:32). It is absolutely essential that we know the truth.

---

11. Jared Sparks, *The Works of Benjamin Franklin* (Boston: Tappan, Whittemore, and Mason, 1840), 10:281–282.

12. John Adams, *The Works of John Adams*, ed. Charles Francis Adams (Boston: Charles Little and James Brown, 1841), 3:421.

Let's take a gander through history for a moment. On February 7, 1954, Rev. George M. Docherty, a pastor of the New York Avenue Presbyterian Church in Washington, D.C. preached a sermon titled "A New Birth of Freedom," while none other than President Dwight D. Eisenhower sat in the audience. In the message, Rev. Docherty suggested that we are a nation "under God" and should be reminded of it daily as our children recite the Pledge of Allegiance. Docherty delivered this message on Lincoln Day, and it had a great impact on those listening—including President Eisenhower, who happened to be seated in the same pew that President Abraham Lincoln had occupied regularly.

A bill was presented to Congress, and on June 14, 1954, just four months later, President Eisenhower signed it into law, officially adding the words "under God" into the Pledge of Allegiance. The president was quoted as saying, "In this way, we are affirming the transcendence of religious faith in America's heritage and future; in this way we shall constantly strengthen those spiritual weapons which forever will be our country's most powerful resource in peace and war." The president then challenged the citizens of this great nation to remember the God of our fathers, for those two words captured "the characteristic and definitive factor in the American way of life." Being a nation "under God" is deeply rooted in our history.

After President Eisenhower signed the bill, some who challenged the modification suggested that Francis Bellamy, the man who wrote the original pledge, would never have agreed to such a change. Yet it was Mr. Bellamy himself who used the phrase many times in 1892. Documents show that Ferdinand used the phrase when writing to Queen Isabella. Captain John Smith used the phrase when writing to Queen Anne. William Bradford, author of the *Mayflower Compact*, also used the phrase frequently when he dedicated America to the "advancement of the Christian faith." More than 21 of the Founding Fathers—including John Hancock, Benjamin Franklin, George Washington, and Thomas Jefferson—used the term "under God" when addressing affairs in America.

The term "under God" dates back to the 13th century when Sir Henry Bracton (ca. 1210–1268), the father of modern law, wrote that the king was "*sub Deo, et Lege*" ("under God and Law")—the phrase etched above the doors at Harvard Law School. This core philosophy of leadership was the basis of contention between Sir Edward Cokes and King James (1620) when the king was reminded that leaders must be accountable to God or nations will fall back into tyranny and justice cannot prevail. This historic dialog is etched on the door of the Supreme Court.

Ultimately, we are a nation that is spiritually, morally, and legally "under God"—and being so is healthy for this generation and the many to come. Those who desire to remove our accountability before Almighty God are the very same people who naïvely believe that a society without religion is a society of free thinkers—a world without restricting boundaries.

Jean Jacque Rousseau (1742) stated that humans are born "inherently good." If this is the case, wouldn't society be better if we could all just explore the potential of humanity in its raw, natural condition and remove the influences of culture and the chains that abound? Ultimately, it always comes back to the idea of removing God from the equation. Well, a nation did remove God, and as a result, 6 million people were murdered with cold and callused resolve from 1933–1945. The Jewish people were slaughtered—men, women and children—at the hands of the Nazi regime.

It was the Nazi perspectives of life that led to the formation of eugenics, a purposeful plan to remove the inferior aspects of humankind and produce the next evolutionary level in humanity. That philosophy still prevails today and was the core worldview of Margaret Sanger (1879–1966), who pioneered reproductive activism and wrote an eight-page monthly newsletter, which circulated throughout greater New York, called "The Rebel Woman—No Gods, No Masters." She founded Planned Parenthood in 1946. Her efforts are directly responsible for the 1.3 million babies murdered every single year. That number is equal to 114,500 monthly; 26,400 weekly; 3,800 daily; roughly 158 per hour; 2.6 babies every second of every day. How is this any different from the gas chambers of Auschwitz, Germany?

When you remove God from the conversation and our accountability to Him, you remove the definitions of morality and the fact that all men were created equal with certain unalienable rights—endowed by a creator. Rather, we become a bio machine to be pruned and prodded until the next cycle in the evolutionary chain takes shape. Having worked at the United Nations, I can tell you that many world leaders share this view. They do not see people as beings created in the image of God. In their minds, we are simply populations of consumers to be manipulated and disposed of. Many leaders consider people to be nothing more than worthless air-breathers consuming the limited natural resources of the planet—contributors to their gross domestic product. Contrary to Jean Jacque Rousseau, power corrupts, and absolute power corrupts absolutely.

We want to believe that deep down inside, people are good, but I am reminded of the wickedness of humankind—the animalistic nature within us—every time I turn on the news. On February 10, 2013, the cruise ship *Carnival Triumph* experienced a fire in the engine room, resulting in the electrical generators breaking down. The ship was left stranded at sea, floating directionless until help could arrive. The systems that provided running water and sewage filtration were limited. Other ships nearby provided food and supplies, but it wasn't long before chaos ensued. The people on board transformed a beautiful cruise into *Lord of the Flies*. Despite the abundance of shelter, food, and supplies, patrons of the floating 4-star resort turned to crime and vandalism. Interior damage to the ship escalated out of control, putting lives in real danger—all due to the lawlessness of those on board. There was no order or accountability. This may be the best social experiment conducted on the human condition in decades. The ship's patrons were stranded for only four days. All was well while the toilets were working, but in 48 hours, there was a total collapse of moral rationale and defining law.

Stories like this remind us once again that people are inherently wicked. In the words of the psalmist, "Surely I was sinful at birth, sinful from the time my mother conceived me" (Psa 51:5). We must heed the words of the prophet Jeremiah who said that people's hearts are "deceitful ... and desperately *wicked*" (Jer 17:9).

I love my children, but had they been born, fed, and left with no direction and then tossed into a room with other children and a box full of toys, you would have witnessed the ugly, sinful nature that flourishes within us all. It is only by God's grace and mercy to teach and instruct us—to set up wise people in positions of authority to establish boundaries—that we have a civilized society at all.

When confronting the evils of the Nazi regime, it was the principles of being a nation "under God" that enabled the prosecution to define right and wrong and the crimes against humanity. At the Nuremberg Trials,[13] Justice Robert H. Jackson set the record straight when he said, "We do not accept the paradox that legal responsibility should be the least where power is the greatest. We stand on the principle of responsible government declared some three centuries ago to King James by Lord Chief Justice Coke, who proclaimed that even a King is still, 'under God and the law.' "[14]

I praise God that our Founding Fathers were devout men of faith. If not for their wisdom and reverence for God, we would have had no laws allowing us to bring justice to those murderers. It was their vision that generations to come would honor God in this way. You need only to pick up the original text of the New England Primer, written in 1687, to see that it was our leaders who wanted all men to read and write, knowing the Scriptures, so they could keep the future leaders of this land accountable to God.

We are one nation under God, and a nation that is under God *must* defend life at all stages—young and old alike—for He values life and desires that all would be saved (1 Tim 2:4). Remember these powerful words and you will always *know it*.

---

13. These took place from November 20, 1945 to October 1, 1946.
14. He spoke these words June 10, 1945.

OWN IT

The Testimony of a Saved Life

Why am I so passionate about the issue of preserving life? Let me begin by taking you back to 1973. During that year, gasoline was 40 cents a gallon, the Sears Tower opened in Chicago, the U.S. withdrew its troops from Vietnam, Skylab was launched into space, Nixon declared "I am not a crook" during the Watergate hearings, Billy Jean King defeated Bobby Riggs during the Battle of the Sexes tennis match, and the Supreme Court rendered a decision on January 22 making abortion a U.S. constitutional right. It was also during this year that the course of my life was dramatically altered—before I had even taken my first breath.

You see, it was in 1973 that my mother, only a teenager at the time, fled for her life. She was running away from the sexual abuse she had endured at the hands of her stepfather. Living in perpetual fear, her only recourse was to run. She made her way to California, where she found a group of other troubled teens. The leader of the pack was a smart but wayward mechanic who was also a drug runner.

Trouble is a magnet for the lost—an oasis to the broken. The group welcomed my mother, and she followed her angry heart into their open arms. The phrase "troubled-youth" does not adequately describe the rebellious outcry that became her defense against vulnerability. In her mind, she would never again be the victim. Yet in the midst of bad choices and a lifestyle that was sure to lead her to prison, she became pregnant. This seems to have been the inevitable outcome of this environment of "free love," with an endless supply of drugs and alcohol.

Like so many others in her position, she made the only choice that seemed right—after all, how could she possibly raise a child when she couldn't feed herself and had little desire to be alive? The man responsible encouraged her to abort the baby, and she did. The affects to her body were harmful. She bled horribly, and the scar tissue was severe. Suddenly aware of the brutal reality that she had just become the victim of her own choices, she cried out to God for help—a God she didn't know and resented.

But this experience didn't stop her from returning to the lifestyle she knew. It wasn't long before she became pregnant again, despite the scar tissue. Shocked and disbelieving, she again followed the harsh advice of the man responsible and returned to the clinic to end this life interruption. But as she contemplated in exasperation, the God she had cried out to answered her. At that moment, she knew she had to take a stand. Perhaps it was the voice of the young Dr. James Dobson on the radio appealing to a society wrought with arrogance and blatant disregard for social responsibility. Perhaps it was the influence of her father, a pastor and police officer, who sought her out and tried to bring hope into her lost life through love and truth. No matter the means, God intervened. My mother made the decision for life and chose to carry her baby to term.

But here is the cold reality: There wasn't a red carpet awaiting her when she returned home that night. There were no flowers in a thoughtfully positioned vase. No, there was only the reality that she was about to become a young mom. She still had no idea how she was going to make it through tomorrow—let alone the next day or the day after that. She had no support and no plan. But that wasn't a problem for the God who had just touched her heart. He was about to make a way in the wilderness.

I praise God for the pregnancy centers across America that help vulnerable women like my mother every single day. They aren't just engaged in the business of saving babies—they are engaged in a business of saving *lives* by reaching out to the moms and dads that society has turned its back against. They are God's hands in action, giving medicine to the brokenhearted and hope to the hopeless.

That's only the beginning of her story. There were still more turns and twists to come, but God was present in each part of her journey. My mother decided it was time to move forward with her life. She moved, took a new job, and tried to create an environment suitable for her new son. She knew the best place for her son was at church. There just happened to be a small but growing church down the road from her new home, Teri Road Baptist Church. She contacted the church, acquired the van schedule, and prepared to send me off to Sunday school the next weekend. As much as she wanted to, she felt that she just couldn't take those first steps into the church herself. She was too ashamed of her past. She was scared she would be judged and confronted, but she didn't want those fears to hold back her son. Her strength and firm resolve against vulnerability would serve her well to push through those tough decisions. So my mother did one of the bravest things I can remember: She walked with me right through the front doors of that little church. And you know what? Not one person put their finger to her chest and judged her for her previous life. No, the body of Christ acted as the body of Christ, welcoming her with open arms.

I don't remember much about Sunday school, but I have fond memories of friends, fun, and stories of hope and redemption. I took home all of my art projects—those illustrated stories of Noah, Moses, and Jesus. My mom would take those projects into her hands, smile, and pull me in with a warm embrace. She would then put magnets to all four corners and proudly display them on the refrigerator. Little did I know that each weekend, those stories were opening her heart to God more and more. At just eight years old, I was an evangelist.

As a result, my mother started attending regularly and gave her heart to Jesus Christ—and I accepted Christ right there with her. Eventually she became the church secretary, planned the youth programs, and even went on to work for Dr. Charles Stanley in Atlanta, Georgia. What a turnaround. Sure, she'd made some mistakes. But God had a greater plan for her life, and she took the baton and ran with it.

***

Fast forward to my young adult life. God was continuing to work in my mother's life. She had renewed her relationship with her father, mother, brother, and sisters, and she was even able to forgive the man who had sexually abused her. You can see why she is one of my heroes. I hope that I have even a fraction of her courage throughout my life. So it breaks my heart to tell you that I went through a rebellious phase. Fortunately, there is a happy ending to this story.

When I was around high school age, my mother—still unmarried—was working hard and doing all she could to put food on the table, pay the bills, and take care of the home. But she was also dating a man I struggled to connect with. He and I were at odds with one another, and I didn't have the heart to bring it up to her. Instead, I got caught up living for myself. I left home before I was 17, which broke my mother's heart. Despite her pleading, I refused to come back. I found my own place, moved in with my girlfriend, Brandi, and we got pregnant.

I remember that Brandi was so distraught by the first pregnancy test. To double check, we consulted the Planned Parenthood brochure we had received at school. We ended up at the clinic, where the nurse suggested that we "terminate" the pregnancy (carefully chosen words). She made a compelling argument, mentioning our youth, our future, our need to go on to college without the burden. Nevertheless, without wavering, Brandi made the choice to carry this baby to term.

All those years at church had made me aware that I was acting in disobedience with my lifestyle. The confirmation that we were pregnant and the reality of the situation drove me to my knees in prayer. I attempted to re-engage the God I had pushed aside. Brandi and I prayed together and started going to church. I reconnected with my mother, and not long after, Brandi and I were in the hospital welcoming our baby girl. Of course, we couldn't have a baby without first being married, so we had an unofficial ceremony to seal the deal. Then, after my wife was able to fit into a wedding dress, we finally had our "official" ceremony in February of 1995.

***

Fast-forward five years. I wish I could say that our trials were behind us. My mother had been through trials, Brandi and I had been through trials, so surely our family was done with all that, right? Well, it doesn't work that way. The enemy is always at work to destroy life. Our next greatest trial was just ahead.

I was in seminary, serving in ministry, and my wife was pregnant with our third child—a baby girl. I was on top of the world. We were on fire for the Lord, I had a beautiful wife, a precious little family, and a daughter on the way—what could possibly go wrong? My wife started having major physical issues. We learned that all the symptoms she was experiencing were caused by an aggressive form of cancer. It had started in her thyroid, spread into her parathyroid glands, throughout her lungs, and into her cervix. When the tests came back, she already had stage 4 cervical cancer.

I remember the conversation like it was yesterday. The doctors wanted us to terminate the pregnancy. She was literally on her deathbed, with potentially 48 hours to live due to her symptoms. The child was at risk, and the mother, my wife, was very much at risk. The doctors wanted to act immediately. "You have too much to live for to test fate," the oncologist told us. I'll not soon forget that feeling of being bullied, of being made to feel like I didn't have a choice in the matter. We were to terminate the pregnancy and begin treatment right away.

My wife and I prayed, and we found another doctor. It wasn't a choice to us. I had to live with the reality that God could take my wife and child to be with Him. I remember vividly telling Brandi, "Either I get to keep you and love on you for all our life together, or you get to go home to Jesus, so you are in a no-lose situation." Brandi was so brave and wouldn't dare agree to abort her child. A work of God was not a choice in her opinion. There was no conversation. Her mind was made up. We gave it to Him in prayer.

When she went to deliver her baby, her cervical cancer was completely gone. It was a miracle. Our little miracle baby entered the world as a testament to the hand of God.

My wife battled cancer for years after, and there were many days of tears, as well as days of rejoicing. The doctors said Brandi would never have another child due to the damage caused by the cancer treatments. She was given a short life expectancy. But God is in the business of proving doctors wrong. Fourteen years later, we have five children, and my wife is strong in both body and spirit.

***

My family's story is still being written, but we know that we have made the right choices—ones that we can live with for all eternity. The enemy tried taking life at every opportunity. He wanted my mother to abort me. He wanted my wife and me to abort our baby girl, and he most certainly wanted us to abort our son, possibly taking my wife in the process. He hates life. But God loves life. He intervened at every turn when we submitted to His will, despite all odds. I am so glad we chose to stay on God's side.

Today, my mother is a devout woman of faith—truly a woman of prayer. She is married to a godly man, and because of her love for God, she has been a blessing to the entire family. Several people, including her mother, have given their lives to Jesus as a result of their relationship with her. Does she still hurt from her pervious decision to take a life? Of course. But God heals and forgives, and He never hated her for her decision. Instead, He bandaged her wounds, gave her love that she had never experienced, and honored His promise to give her a hope and future (Jer 29:11).

Just look at what God has done! In the midst of tragedy, one choice—a choice for life—was the first step on a path to complete transformation. That child that almost wasn't, that almost-notch in Margaret Sanger's belt, that "inconvenience," is now a husband, father of five, pastor, teacher, ministry leader, and more importantly, a devoted servant of Jesus Christ.

God took what the enemy had planned for evil and turned it to good. He stopped the lava flow, and from the crusted surface, He brought forth a sprout of hope and restoration in my family legacy. Every conception is a life with limitless potential in the hands of a Holy God.

I shouldn't be here today. My whole life is a miracle. And guess what? So is yours. That's why this chapter is titled "Own It." We all have a testimony, and like it or not, we have all been affected by decisions to take the life of the unborn. I am a pastor who was one decision away from never giving a sermon. Every child is a member of our society, and abortion denies them the God-given opportunity to add their brushstroke on the tapestry of life.

We have to own the fact that when we made a decision for Christ, we embarked on a new path that puts the world behind us and the cross before us. We are no longer our own. We belong to Him. That means we must take responsibility for the impact our decisions are making on the future generations. We must own up to what is happening on our watch at this very moment. This is not someone else's problem—it is our responsibility. We must not sleep until we have done all we can to alter the course of a society on the verge of genocide and self-destruction. Now it is time to *live it*.

LIVE IT

Understanding Our Role to Defend the Defenseless

Alice Paul spoke well when she said, "Abortion is the ultimate exploitation of women." The psychological and physical effects of abortion on women are devastating, and the residual impact an abortion has on the dynamics of their future relationships and interactions is immense. You can't take a life by the blade of a knife and remain unscathed. Although Pontius Pilate didn't carry out the execution of Jesus that he granted, Jesus' blood was as much on his hands as those who carried out the assignment— if not more. And the blood of more than 55 million babies is on our hands.

Children are dying on our watch as we sit by hoping that someone else will stand in the gap. But we have been called for such a time as this. We are completely equipped in Christ to step up now and make a difference that will affect generations to come.

Over 41 years ago, a young, pregnant woman named Norma McCorvey played an instrumental role in the Supreme Court decision that brought legal abortion to America. McCorvey is the *Roe* in the *Roe v. Wade* case. Now, having given her life to the Lord in 1995, McCorvey is campaigning to save babies. God is using her testimony to save lives.

Imagine the impact your life can have on society. In his essay "Christian Behavior," C. S. Lewis writes, "If you read history you will find that the Christians who did most for the present world were precisely those who thought most of the next. ... It is since Christians have largely ceased to think of the other world that they have become so ineffective in this."[1] Sacrificing the temporal for the eternal is what separates the wheat from the chaff (Matt 3:12). There is no room for lukewarm believers in God's kingdom. As Revelation 3:16 states, "Because you are lukewarm, and neither hot nor cold, I will spit you out of My mouth" (NASB).

God wants our very best—He wants our all. If we do not stand up for life, who will? If you do not hold the line, who will? In his book *Crazy Love*, Francis Chan illustrates what this means:

> When I was in high school, I seriously considered joining the Marines; this was when they first came out with the commercials for "the few, the proud, the Marines." But you know what? I didn't bother to ask if they would modify the rules for me so I could run less, and maybe also do fewer push-ups. That would've been pointless and stupid, and I knew it. Everyone knows that if you sign up for the Marines, you have to do whatever they tell you. They own you. Somehow this realization does not cross over to our thinking about the Christian life. Jesus didn't say that

---

1. C.S. Lewis, *Mere Christianity* (New York: Harper Collind, 1952), 134

if you wanted to follow Him you could do it in a lukewarm manner. He said, "Take up your cross and follow me."[2]

Either you're going to stand boldly for the Lord or you're not. Christ interacted with people who were too comfortable with their lives, and He challenged them. He told a son to leave his family and follow Him (Matt 8:21–22). He told a wealthy man that to follow Him would mean total sacrifice, stressing that even the Son of Man didn't have a pillow to lay His head upon (Matt 8:18–20). He told another that he should sell all that he had and give to the poor (Matt 19:16–30). In each case, these eager men were cut to their heart because they wanted to be good but not great. They weren't willing to go all the way.

Jesus promises a reward for full commitment: "And everyone who has left houses or brothers or sisters or father or mother or wife or children or fields for my sake will receive a hundred times as much and will inherit eternal life" (Matt 19:29–30). He is not asking us to ditch our families in this statement. Rather, He is challenging us to look inward to truly examine and evaluate our priorities. Is there something that you hold in higher regard or value than your love for God? What you find in your heart may hurt a little when you consider the true cost of following Christ.

The world is restless, and only God's people, in humble petition for revival, will make a difference. As a pastor, I am witnessing a vast departure from the spiritual starvation that has left people hungering for the rich, deep truth of the Scripture—a return to the ideas of what it means to take up the cross and follow Him. Resonating with the powerful words of Francis Chan and David Platt, there is a transformation in the culture,

2. Francis Chan, *Crazy Love* (Colorado Springs: David C. Cook, 2008), 80.

with masses stepping out of the lukewarm waters of diluted, self-help Christianity into a solemn assembly and sacrificial devotion to the King of kings. The revelation of our own depravity from years of lip service has finally brought to light the words of Isaiah 29:13 and Matthew 15:8: "These people come near to me with their mouth and honor me with their lips, but their hearts are far from me."

There is no room for secular Christianity. As E. M. Bounds stated in his powerful book *The Weapon of Prayer*,

> A breed of Christian is greatly needed who will seek tirelessly after God, who will give Him no rest, day and night, until He hearken to their cry. The times demand praying men and women who are all athirst for God's glory, who are broad and unselfish in their desires, quenchless for God, who seek Him late and early, and who will give themselves no rest until the whole earth be filled with His glory.[3]

The cultural chasm is growing wider between those who claim their devotion to Christ and those who are choosing the path of the world. It is time for people to decide to whom they will give their allegiance—and, indeed, the time grows short. The hour of decision is upon us, and it is one of eternal consequence. When the heat turns up in this society—and it most certainly will—are you going to be willing to walk into the furnace for your faith (Dan 3:1–29)? The Holy Spirit will give you strength when that moment comes, but *you* must take the first step (Acts 7:54–60).

---

3. Edward M. Bounds, *The Weapon of Prayer* (Grand Rapids, MI: Baker Book House, 1991), 30.

Are you willing to step into the lion's den for God (Dan 6:1–23)? When you take a stand for the Lord and His love for life, get ready for a blast of lion's breath because according to Scripture, the enemy is a roaring lion (1 Pet 5:8). But take heart—we face a defeated enemy. Let him roar all he wants to. After a while, his growl will weaken, and you will no longer be intimidated by a losing foe. Adrian Rogers said, "Satan's real war is not with you … it is with God. Evil persons have always known that if they cannot harm someone directly, harm someone that they love, and you've hurt them. Satan's war is with God, but he has set his attack on you because God has set His affection on you."[4] Satan wants you in a constant state of fear because he wants you to begin to doubt God's provision, promises, and love for you.

The Call

You have a decision to make. You have invested time into reading the words before you. You may take these words to heart, allowing them to reshape your prayer life, the way you spend your resources, the way you vote, the way you prioritize, the way you live—and especially your views toward defending life at all stages. Or you may choose to tune them out and go about your daily existence. You may suddenly feel pressed, even guilty, by the overwhelming feeling that God has burdened you with information that presents a seemingly daunting assignment—one that forces you to make immediate changes. Perhaps you weren't ready for that. Well, whether you're ready or not, God wants to use you.

---

4. Adrian Rogers, "The Full Armor of God," audio recording, accessed August 18, 2008.

Let me paint a picture for you of the kind of people God uses to bring about His will.[5] Moses played one of the most vital roles in the redemption of humanity. As the administrator and enforcer of the law, he enacted a system that would not be fulfilled until 1,550 years later by God's perfect design. But Moses wasn't initially willing to assume this role.

God had selected Moses from birth to save the nation of Israel and lead His people into the promised land. When Moses was an infant, God saved him from death at the hands of the Egyptians, instead orchestrating events so that Moses was taken into Pharaoh's palace to be raised as royalty. Despite his lofty position, Moses identified with and cared for his people. One day, after witnessing an Egyptian abuse a fellow Hebrew, Moses killed the Egyptian and buried his body in the sand (Exod 2:11–12). He then fled to Midian, where he married and started a family.

By now, Moses was approximately 40 years old. He had a new home, a family, and was making a living tending sheep. It was at this point that God chose to act. Speaking to Moses from a burning bush, God called him to do what had never been done: deliver an entire nation from slavery and oppression. Moses should have been eager to do whatever God asked of him—after all, he owed his very life to God. But the biblical account shows that Moses was more than a little reluctant to accept the role God had for him.

Instead of agreeing to God's plan in humility and obedience, Moses insisted that he was the wrong man for the job, saying, "Who am I, that I should go to Pharaoh and bring the Israelites

---

5. The material in this section is adapted from my book *The Front Line: A Prayer Warrior's Guide to Spiritual Battle* (Bellingham, WA: Kirkdale Press, 2012).

out of Egypt?" (Exod 3:11). God assured Moses of His presence, promising him a sign, telling Moses His name, and describing the miracles He would perform to make the Egyptians listen. But Moses continued asking questions: "What if they do not believe me or listen to me and say, 'The LORD did not appear to you'?" (Exod 4:1). In response, God gave Moses two miraculous signs to perform.

Despite God's assurances, signs, and promises, Moses continued to make excuses, replying, "Pardon your servant, Lord. I have never been eloquent, neither in the past nor since you have spoken to your servant. I am slow of speech and tongue" (Exod 4:10). God assured Moses that He would give him the words to speak and teach him what to say, but Moses again tried to convince God that he was not the man for the job: "Pardon your servant, Lord. Please send someone else" (Exod 4:13). In anger, God proposed yet another solution: He would have Aaron come alongside Moses to speak for him, but Moses would still perform the miracles God had given him. Moses finally relented, agreeing to obey the Lord's command, and the rest is history.

Why did Moses resist obeying God's command? He was afraid, unwilling to adjust his life to God's plan, and in great doubt of his own ability. But God wasn't asking Moses to perform this feat in his own ability or strength, only to be an instrument in His hand.

God's Standards

Like Moses, many of God's chosen people throughout Scripture were fearful. They were not machines, impervious to human emotion. Christ Himself suffered from the fear of torture and pain that He would experience on the cross. In the midst of His anguish, He prayed, "Father, if you are willing, take this cup from me" (Luke 22:42). Even Elijah, a mighty prophet of the Lord, was overwhelmed with fear when Jezebel put a bounty on his head: "Elijah was afraid and ran for his life. … He came to a broom bush, sat down under it and prayed that he might die. 'I have had enough, LORD,' he said. 'Take my life; I am no better than my ancestors'" (1 Kgs 19:3–5). Genesis 32:1–12 shows Jacob trembling in fear in anticipation of meeting his brother, Esau, for the first time since stealing his birthright and blessing. Yet on this same journey, Jacob wrestled fearlessly with the living God and received a blessing.

Hebrews 11, also known as the "faith chapter," tells of men and women of faith who stood firm in the face of persecution and death, even though they never saw God's promises come to pass in their lifetimes. Yet each of these faithful believers had weaknesses, made mistakes, and experienced fear and other human emotions even though they had faith in God.

God often selects men and women who appear unqualified in the eyes of the world to perform great and mighty deeds in His power. David is a case in point. When Samuel, working on God's instructions, sought a new king to replace Saul, God told him, "The LORD does not look at the things man looks at. People look at the outward appearance, but the LORD looks at the heart" (1 Sam 16:7). Samuel suspected that God had chosen one of David's tall, well-spoken, distinguished-looking brothers. Instead, God chose David, the young shepherd boy. David went on to become one of the greatest kings the world has ever known.

The disciples that Christ hand-picked were looked down upon because they were not educated men. But because they had no personal claim to their knowledge or authority, they were able to exalt Christ and His authority in their testimony about Him. Their weakness was their strength.

God's standards for choosing His servants are different than our own. As the Apostle Paul writes,

> Brothers, think of what you were when you were called. Not many of you were wise by human standards; not many were influential; not many were of noble birth. But God chose the foolish things of the world to shame the wise; God chose the weak things of the world to shame the strong. He chose the lowly things of this world and the despised things—and the things that are not—to nullify the things that are, so that no one may boast before him (1 Cor 1:26–29).

When Moses laid his fears before the Lord, he was speaking on our behalf. Each of us would have trembled as well at the Lord's assignment. Moses was just bold enough (or scared enough) to voice what we ourselves would have felt. The same is true for other biblical heroes. They all had fears and doubts, but God was their strength and confidence. When we look at their accomplishments, we know that God—not education, heritage, wealth, or stature—was the source of their power. If God could use these men, He can use us.

Call to Action

In Christ, we are cleansed and forgiven, thoroughly equipped through the Holy Spirit to do mighty things for God. I praise God for those who have stood boldly in the face of injustice to defend the defenseless at great personal sacrifice. By God's equipping power, we have seen abortion clinics closing up shop and lives saved. In 1992 there were 2,100 abortion clinics in America; by the 40th anniversary of the *Roe v. Wade* decision, there were just over 600 clinics remaining. Yet that is still far too many. Babies are being killed daily.

You can make a difference, as countless individuals already have. Mark Crutcher, president of Life Dynamics Incorporated, emphasizes the impact that the fight for life has already had on society. He writes,

> If the pro-life movement had never existed, every public school and university in America would either have an on-site abortion clinic or a contract with a nearby abortionist. ... There would be no debate about taxpayer funding of abortion; the government would have been forcing us to pay for them since day one. ... The right-to-life of the unborn would not even be discussed in either the public arena or the political process. ... Poll after poll would not be documenting a dramatic shift away from support for legalized abortion and toward the pro-life position— especially among the young. ... We would not see the precious faces of children with disabilities like Down syndrome—not because these maladies had been cured but because abortion would have long ago become the accepted medical "treatment" for every "imperfect" baby. After all, killing people is easier than healing or accommodating them. ... There would be no crisis pregnancy network to help those women who might not want to submit to abortion. That's because, without your voice, abortion would be the default position for every unplanned pregnancy.[6]

6. Mark Crutcher, "Reflection and Perspective," *Unique Perspectives on the Battle for Life* (blog), January 25, 2013, http://markcrutcherblog.com/index. cfm/2013/1/.

Our country would be a very different place if it were not for the pro-life movement and those individuals who answered the call rather than leaving their watchmen duties to another. Mark Crutcher declares that without the work of brave souls who have fought to preserve life, "America would have devolved into a country where the killing of an unborn child has no more moral significance than the pulling of a tooth."[7]

God is calling on you to be bold and courageous in a world that is destitute. When you fight in the strength of the Lord, you'll be willing to attack the first of hell with water pistols (Phil 4:13) because mountains move through His mighty hand. When Elisha told the Israelites in 2 Kings 3 that the Lord was about to answer their prayers, despite their disobedience, he called them to grab shovels. They prayed for water, and God instructed them to dig. When they had filled the valley with ditches, the Lord filled the dry wells with more water than they could imagine.

To receive God's bountiful blessings, sometimes we have to dig—to labor. Grab a shovel, and let's get to work. Stay the course, keep up the good fight, and together we will see the end of abortion in America and any law that would dare treat life at any stage as expendable. We must hold the line. It is time to *live it.*

---

7. Crutcher, "Reflection and Perspective."

THE CASE FOR LIFE

By Rob Schwarzwalder and Cathy Cleaver Ruse
of the Family Research Council[1]

Abortion is unlike any other issue debated today. Millions of American women have aborted a child, and the pain, loss, and emotional need to justify what was done—both on the part of the mother and on the part of her loved ones—is strong and deep.[2] This means that, in any debate, you may face an invisible thumb on the scale so that even the best logic will fail to persuade.

The best you can do is arm yourself with the facts and deliver them in what you hope will be a winning way for your audience—meaning you will need to make your case, in most

---

1. This content is also available online; see Rob Schwarzwalder and Cathy Cleaver Ruse, "The Best Pro-Life Arguments for Secular Audiences," Family Research Council, http://downloads.frc.org/EF/EF11J30.pdf. The authors would like to thank Eliza Thurston for her research assistance.

2. Many individuals are suffering because of abortion and do not know where to turn for help. If you are interacting with such a person, mention that many people have found hope and healing after abortion through programs like Project Rachel, established by the Catholic Church to serve all people regardless of religious affiliation. If you mention this program and its website (www.hopeafterabortion.com) in passing, you can impart life-saving information without coming across as proselytizing.

instances, not in the language of faith or religion but in the language of the post-modern secularist.

What follows are the best arguments from science, the law, and women's rights to advance the pro-life case against abortion.

Arguing from Science

The "classic" arguments from the other side are collapsing under the weight of science. The arguments that "No one knows when life begins" and "It's a blob of tissue" are on the wane, especially in the context of surgical abortion, which is how the vast majority of abortions are done today.[3]

Still, establishing the evidence of the beginnings of human life will ground your argumentation in science, giving you a firm foundation for additional arguments and preempting the charge that you are basing your position on faith or religious belief.

Cite the Facts

Here is a thumbnail sketch of the scientific evidence of the existence of human life before birth. These are irrefutable facts, about which there is no dispute in the scientific community.[4]

At the moment when a human sperm penetrates a human ovum, or egg, which generally takes place in the upper portion of

---

3. These arguments are still used in debates over early abortion pills and embryo-destructive research.

4. We will not discuss fetal pain because the time at which a child in the womb can experience pain is hotly disputed, and the aim of this work is to present only undisputed facts so that a persuasive argument can be made without the distraction of a contest over facts. To read more about fetal pain, see Ashley Morrow Fragoso, "Fetal Pain: Can Unborn Children Feel Pain in the Womb?" Family Research Council, 2010, http://downloads.frc.org/EF/EF10H06.pdf.

the Fallopian tube, a new entity comes into existence. "Zygote" is the name of the first cell formed at conception, the earliest developmental stage of the human embryo. This is followed by the "morula" and "blastocyst" stages.[5] Is it human? Is it alive? Is it just a cell, or is it an actual organism—a "being"? These are logical questions. You should raise them, and then provide the answers.

Is it human?

The zygote is composed of human DNA and other human molecules, so its nature is undeniably human, not some other species. The new human zygote has a genetic composition that is absolutely unique, different from any other human that has ever existed, including that of its mother (thus disproving the claim that only "a woman and her body" are involved in abortion.[6] This DNA includes a complete "design" that guides not only early development but even hereditary attributes that will appear in childhood and adulthood, from hair and eye color to personality traits.[7]

Is it alive?

The earliest human embryo is biologically alive. It fulfills the four criteria needed to establish biological life: metabolism, growth, reaction to stimuli, and reproduction.[8]

---

5. Marjorie A. England, "What Is An Embryo?" in *Life Before Birth* (London: Mosby-Wolfe, 1996).
6. Keith L. Moore and T.V.N. Persaud, *The Developing Human: Clinically Oriented Embryology* (Philadelphia: W.B. Saunders Co., 1998), 77, 350.
7. Ibid.
8. Carl Sagan, *Billions and Billions* (New York: Random House, 1997), 163–179. See *The American Heritage Medical Dictionary*: "The property or quality that distinguishes living organisms from dead organisms and inanimate

Is it just a cell, or is it an actual organism—a "being"?

Scientists define an organism as a complex structure of interdependent elements constituted to carry on the activities of life by separately-functioning but mutually dependent organs.[9] The human zygote meets this definition with ease. Once formed, it initiates a complex sequence of events to ready it for continued development and growth. The zygote acts immediately and decisively to initiate a program of development that will, if uninterrupted by accident, disease, or external intervention, proceed seamlessly through formation of the definitive body, birth, childhood, adolescence, maturity, and aging, ending with death. This coordinated behavior is the very hallmark of an organism.[10]

By contrast, while a mere collection of human cells may carry on the activities of cellular life, it will not exhibit coordinated interactions directed toward a higher level of organization.[11]

The scientific evidence is quite plain: At the moment of fusion of human sperm and egg, a new entity comes into

---

matter, manifested in functions such as metabolism, growth, reproduction, and response to stimuli or adaptation to the environment originating from within the organism." *The American Heritage Medical Dictionary*, reprint edition (May 7, 2008), s.v. "Life."

9. For more on the definition of an organism, see MedlinePlus, the online health information service of the National Institutes of Health: *MedlinePlus/Merriam-Webster Online*, s.v. "Organism," accessed January 21, 2011 , http://www.merriam-webster.com/medlineplus/organism.

10. Maureen L. Condic, "When Does Human Life Begin? A Scientific Perspective," The Westchester Institute for Ethics and the Human Person, *Westchester Institute White Paper Series* 1, no. 1 (October 2008): 7. Full article available at: http://www.westches-terinstitute.net/resources/white-papers/351-white-paper.

11. Ibid., 7.

existence that is distinctly human, alive, and an individual organism—a living, and fully human, being.[12]

Prepare for Common Pro-Choice Responses

Some defenders of abortion will concede the scientific proofs but will argue that the entity in the womb is still not, or not yet, a *person*. This is a decidedly unscientific argument: It has nothing to do with science and everything to do with someone's own moral or political philosophy. If you encounter such an argument, it is a good time to recite the scientific proofs and maybe make a philosophical point of your own: We're either persons or property. Even the staunchest abortion defender will be reluctant to call a human child a piece of property.[13]

Others may suggest that humanness depends on something spiritual, like infusion of a soul. However, to argue there is no soul until birth or some other time is, by definition, to argue something incapable of proof. This argument presents another good opportunity to recite the scientific proofs.

While the science on when life begins is clear, some still claim that *pregnancy* doesn't begin until the embryo implants

---

12. As a general proposition, every human being comes into existence by the fusion of a human egg with a human sperm, but twinning can result in multiple children from one human egg, and there is the potential for cloning of a human embryo. See Judith G. Hall, "Twinning," *The Lancet*, 362 (August 20, 2003): 735–43. See also National Institutes of Health, Stem Cell Information Glossary, s.v. "Somatic cell nuclear transfer (SCNT)," accessed March 15, 2011, http://stemcells.nih.gov/StemCells/Templates/ StemCellContentPage.aspx?NRMODE=Published&NRNODEGUID={3C35 BAB 6-0FE6-4C4E-95F2-2CB61B58D96D}&NRORIGINAL URL=%2finfo%2fglossary.asp&NRCACHEHINT =NoModifyGuest#scnt.
13. For more on this theme, see Sam Brownback and Jim Nelson Black, *From Power to Purpose: A Remarkable Journey of Faith and Compassion* (Nashville: Thomas Nelson, 2007), 44.

itself in the lining of the uterine wall, which occurs about a week later. Why? Politics and profit. Acceptance of an implantation-based definition of pregnancy would allow abortion providers to mischaracterize pills and technologies that work after conception but before implantation as "contraception," making them potentially less subject to regulation and more acceptable and attractive to consumers. The Guttmacher Institute[14] and the American College of Obstetricians and Gynecologists, two institutes who support legalized abortion have pushed for this type of pregnancy redefinition for decades.

If your interlocutor raises this issue, point out that the word "contraception" literally means "against conception"; therefore, something cannot be said to be a "contraceptive" if it allows conception. Also point out that the fertilization-based definition of pregnancy is still the predominant definition in medical dictionaries today.[15]

Cite More Facts on Human Development

Human beings develop at an astonishingly rapid pace. Giving a quick recitation of the child's development will weaken the "not a person yet" mentality.

- The cardiovascular system is the first major system to function. At about 22 days after conception, the child's

---

14. The abortion research institute originally established by the Planned Parenthood Federation of America

15. For more on this topic, see Christopher M. Gacek, "Conceiving 'Pregnancy': U.S. Medical Dictionaries and Their Definitions of 'Conception' and 'Pregnancy'," Family Research Council (April 2009), accessed March 16, 2011, http://downloads.frc.org/EF/EF09D12.pdf. See also Robert G. Marshall and Charles A. Donovan, *Blessed Are the Barren: The Social Policy of Planned Parenthood* (San Francisco: Ignatius Press, 1991), 291–302.

heart begins to circulate his own blood, unique to that of his mother's, and his heartbeat can be detected on ultrasound.[16]

- At just six weeks, the child's eyes and eyelids, nose, mouth, and tongue have formed.

- Electrical brain activity can be detected at six or seven weeks,[17] and by the end of the eighth week, the child, now known scientifically as a "fetus," has developed all of his organs and bodily structures.[18]

- By 10 weeks after conception the child can make bodily movements.

Today, parents can see the development of their children with their own eyes. The obstetric ultrasound done typically at 20 weeks gestation provides not only pictures but a real-time video of the active life of the child in the womb: clasping his hands, sucking his thumb, yawning, stretching, getting the hiccups, covering his ears to a loud sound nearby[19]—even smiling.[20]

---

16. Moore and Persaud, *The Developing Human*, 350–358.

17. The Commission of Inquiry into Foetal Sentience (CARE and The House of Lords), "Human Sentience Before Birth" (2001): 3, 36.

18. England, *Life Before Birth*, 9.

19. See "Fetal Development," MedlinePlus, accessed January 21, 2011, http://www.nlm.nih.gov/medline-plus/ency/article/002398.htm; and "Your Pregnancy Week by Week: Weeks 17–20," WebMD, accessed March 15, 2011, http://www.webmd.com/baby/ guide/your-pregnancy-week-by-week-weeks-17-20?page=2.

20. Sophie Borland, "The foetus who broke into a big smile...aged only 17 weeks," *Daily Mail*, October 11, 2010, accessed April 4, 2011, http://www. dai-lymail.co.uk/health/article-1319373/The-foetus-broke-big-smile--aged-17-weeks.html.

Medicine, too, confirms the existence of the child before birth as a distinct human person. Fetal surgery has become a medical specialty and includes the separate provision of anesthesia to the baby. You can cite some of the surgeries now performed on children before their birth, such as shunting to bypass an obstructed urinary tract, removal of tumors at the base of the tailbone, and treatment of congenital heart disease.[21]

If these arguments don't persuade your audience, consider citing authorities from the "pro-choice"[22] community itself. Mention pro-choice feminist Naomi Wolf, who, in a groundbreaking article in 1996, argued that the abortion-rights community should acknowledge the "fetus, in its full humanity" and that abortion causes "a real death."[23] More recently, Kate Michelman, long-time president of NARAL Pro-Choice America, acknowledged that "technology has clearly helped to define how people think about a fetus as a full, breathing human being."[24]

---

21. Aetna, Inc., "Clinical Policy Bulletin: Fetal Surgery In Utero," *Aetna Insurance Clinical Policy Bulletin* (last revised October 2010), accessed January 21, 2011, http://www.aetna.com/cpb/medical/data/400_499/0449.html.
22. In an abortion debate, the importance of language cannot be understated. Many in the pro-life movement prefer to use the term "pro-abortion" to describe those who support the legalization of abortion. But use of this term may unduly antagonize your interlocutor and risk shutting down debate. By using the term "pro-choice" in quotation marks, you are signaling that this is what the other side calls itself. It is also an extension of goodwill, and you should ask for the same courtesy.
23. Naomi Wolf, "Our Bodies, Our Souls," *The New Republic*, October 16, 1995, 26–35.
24. Sarah Kliff, "Remember *Roe!*" *Newsweek*, April 16, 2010, accessed February 28, 2011, http://www.news-week.com/2010/04/15/remember-roe.html.

Arguing from the Law

Ultimately, those who justify abortion by claiming that "no one knows when life begins" are not arguing science; rather, they're arguing their own brand of politics, philosophy, or even religion. Their argument is not about when life begins but about when, or whether, that life deserves legal acknowledgment and protection. That brings us to our next topic: the law.

Understanding *Roe v. Wade*

Most people do not really know what the Supreme Court decided on January 22, 1973. They assume that the court made abortion legal in the first trimester of pregnancy only, and that it is subject to substantial limits and regulations today. You will be able to change minds when you inform them that neither of these assumptions is true.

The Supreme Court in *Roe v. Wade* did not create a limited right to abortion but a virtually unlimited right to abortion throughout pregnancy. The case involved an 1854 Texas law prohibiting abortion except "for the purpose of saving the life of the mother." The plaintiff, whose real name is Norma McCorvey, desired a purely elective abortion and filed suit claiming the Texas law deprived her of constitutional rights.

Seven members of the Supreme Court agreed. While admitting that abortion is not in the text of the Constitution, they nevertheless ruled that a right to abortion was part of an implied "right to privacy" that the Court had fashioned in previous rulings regarding contraception regulations.[25] They also

---

25. "Privacy" is not in the text of the Constitution either.

ruled that the word "person" in the Constitution did not include a fetus.[26]

For a debate on abortion policy, the most important part of the ruling to understand is the new law it established. Commit this description to memory: The court ruled that abortion must be permitted for any reason a woman chooses until the child becomes viable; after viability, an abortion must still be permitted if an abortion doctor deems the abortion necessary to protect a woman's "health,"[27] defined by the court in another ruling issued the same day as "all factors—physical, emotional, psychological, familial, and the woman's age—relevant to the well-being of the patient."[28]

In this way, the court created a right to abort a child at any time, even past the point of viability, for "emotional" reasons. Stated another way, the Supreme Court gave abortion doctors the power to override any abortion restriction merely by claiming that there are emotional reasons for the abortion. Abortion advocates want to hide this, but liberal journalists such as David Savage of the *Los Angeles Times* have reported the truth about *Roe*, saying the Supreme Court created an "absolute right to abortion" under which "any abortion can be justified."[29]

---

26. *Roe v. Wade*, 410 U.S. 113, 153–163 (1973).

27. Roe at 162–65. "If the State is interested in protecting fetal life after viability, it may go so far as to pro-scribe abortion during that period, except when it is necessary to preserve the life *or health* of the mother." Ibid., 163–64 (emphasis added).

28. *Doe v. Bolton*, 410 U.S. 179, 192 (1973). The court in *Roe* said: "That opinion [Doe v. Bolton] and this one, of course, are to be read together." *Roe* at 165.

29. David G. Savage, "*Roe* Ruling: More Than Its Author Intended," *Los Angeles Times*, September 14, 2005, accessed January 21, 2011, http://articles. lat-imes.com/2005/sep/14/nation/na-abortion14.

Constructing a Pro-Life Legal Argument

Explain what Roe means

When you make the pro-life case, explain the basics of the actual ruling and then cite the David Savage quote that *Roe* created an "absolute right to abortion" under which "any abortion can be justified." Chances are, your audience will not know that the court created an unlimited right to abortion, and odds are good that they won't agree with it. They are not alone. Lydia Saad, senior editor for the Gallup polling company, which has long tracked abortion opinion, states, "Most Americans favor legal restrictions on abortion that go way beyond current law."[30]

The way Americans self-identify has changed dramatically over the years. In the mid-1990s, "pro-life" was a distinct minority view. But in May 2009, for the first time, a significantly greater percentage of Americans self-identified as "pro-life" than "pro-choice."[31]

Be prepared to cite these and other public opinion polls from various organizations

- Sixty-one percent of Americans say abortion should be illegal after the fetal heartbeat has begun,[32] which occurs in the first month of pregnancy.

---

30. Lydia Saad, "The New Normal on Abortion: Americans More Pro-Life," Gallup, May 14, 2010, accessed March 16, 2011, http://www.gallup.com/poll/128036/New-Normal-Abortion-Americans-Pro-Life.aspx. See William McGurn, " Gallup's Pro-Life America," *Wall Street Journal*, June 1, 2010, accessed March 14, 2011, http://online.wsj.com/ar-ticle/SB1000142405274870 459650457527278010432 9228.html.
31. Gallup Poll, May 7–9, 2009.
32. Zogby International Poll, April 15–17, 2004.

- Seventy-two percent of Americans say abortion should be illegal after the first three months of pregnancy.[33]

- Eighty-six percent of Americans say abortion should be illegal after the first six months of pregnancy.[34]

- Only six to seventeen percent of Americans (depending on how the question is asked and by whom) believe abortion should be legal at any time, in all circumstances.[35]

One of the best surveys to have in your arsenal was conducted by the Center for Gender Equality, run by former Planned Parenthood President Faye Wattleton. Its 2003 nationwide survey of women revealed that a majority of women (51 percent) believe abortion should either never be permitted or permitted only for rape, incest, or life endangerment.[36] That means a

---

33. Humphrey Taylor, "The Harris Poll #18," Harris Interactive, Inc., March 3, 2005.

34. Ibid.

35. This last point is crucial, as it means only a small minority of Americans agree with Roe. A recent Marist Poll/Knights of Columbus survey found that only 6% of Americans believe "abortion should be available to a woman any time she wants one during her entire pregnancy." See "Abortion in America," Marist Poll/Knights of Columbus, July 2009, accessed March 16, 2011, http://www. kofc.org/un/en/news/releases/detail/548612.html. Another survey found that 17% believe "abortion should be legal in all cases." See "Religion and the Issues: Results from the 2010 Annual Religion and Public Life Survey," Pew Forum on Religion and Public Life, September 17, 2010 (17% believe "abortion should be legal in all cases"), accessed March 16, 2011, http://pewforum.org/uploadedFiles/Top-ics/Issues/Politics_and_Elections/immigration-en-vironment-views-fullreport.pdf.

36. Seventeen percent (17%) said abortion should never be permitted; 34% said abortion should be permitted only for rape, incest, or life endangerment. See Princeton Survey Research Associates on behalf of the Center for Gender

majority of women believe abortion should be permitted only in extremely rare circumstances.[37] What's more, when asked to rank the top priorities for the women's movement, the women ranked "Keeping abortion legal" next to last, just before "More girls in sports."[38]

Cite Criticism of Roe from Pro-Choice Sources

You can also cite a long and growing list of prominent pro-choice legal commentators who call *Roe v. Wade* indefensible. The late John Hart Ely of Yale, for instance, argued that *Roe* was wrong "because it is not constitutional law and gives almost no sense of an obligation to try to be."[39] The law clerk of Justice Blackmun, who authored the *Roe v. Wade* opinion, calls it "one of the most intellectually suspect constitutional decisions of the

---

Equality, "Progress and Perils: How Gender Issues Unite and Divide Women, Part Two," (April 7, 2003): 9–10.

37. Rape/incest abortions account for only one percent of abortions every year according to the Guttmacher Institute, and life-saving abortions are similarly rare. See Lawrence B. Finer et al., "Reasons U.S. Women Have Abortions: Quantitative and Qualitative Perspectives," *Perspectives on Sexual and Reproductive Health* 37, no. 5 (2005): 113–14. This survey shows that only -0.5% of women report that their abortion was because they were "a victim of rape" and only -0.5% report that their abortion was because they "became pregnant as a result of incest." To determine the number of abortions done to save the life of the mother, see data collected by the Centers for Medicare & Medicaid Services, U.S. Department of Health and Human Services, which show a drop in Medicaid-funded abortions by over 99% —from 294,600 in Fiscal Year 1977 to fewer than 1,000 in FY 1982 and subsequent years—after the federal Medicaid program began funding only abortions to save the mother's life.

38. *Progress and Perils*, 4.

39. John Hart Ely, "The Wages of Crying Wolf: A Comment on Roe v. Wade," *The Yale Law Journal*, 82 (1973): 920–949.

modern era."[40] The legal editor of the *Washington Post* says it has "a deep legitimacy problem."[41] Even Justice Ruth Bader Ginsburg has been critical of *Roe*, saying that it "ventured too far in the change it ordered and presented an incomplete justification for its action."[42] She also stated that the *Roe* decision was "not the way courts generally work."[43]

Cite Abortion Incidence

You should also have at the ready this shocking fact from the Guttmacher Institute about abortion incidence in America: The United States has the highest abortion rate in the western world and the third-highest abortion rate of all developed nations worldwide.[44] Cite this statistic and its source whenever you speak about abortion law in America.

Discuss Elective Abortion

Another important statistic that you should always cite is also from the Guttmacher Institute. In the last 25 years, Guttmacher has conducted two major studies asking women why they chose abortion. Their answers have remained basically the same: Only

40. Edward Lazarus, "The Lingering Problems with Roe v. Wade," *FindLaw Legal Commentary*, October 3, 2002, accessed January 21, 2011, http://writ.corporate.findlaw.com/lazarus/20021003.html.

41. Benjamin Wittes, "Letting Go of Roe," *The Atlantic Monthly*, January/February 2005, 48.

42. Ruth Bader Ginsburg, "Some Thoughts on Autonomy and Equality in Relation to Roe v. Wade," *North Carolina Law Review* 63 (1985): 376.

43. Ruth Bader Ginsburg, "A Conversation with Justice Ruth Bader Ginsburg," *University of Kansas Law Review* 53 (June 2005): 962.

44. Gilda Sedgh et al., "Legal Abortion Worldwide: Incidence and Recent Trends," *International Family Planning Perspectives*, 33 (September 2007): 108. Full report available as: http://www.guttmacher.org/pubs/journals/3310607.html

seven percent of women report that their abortion was because of a health reason or a possible health problem with the baby, and less than half a percent report that their abortion was because they became pregnant as a result of rape. Ninety-two percent of abortions in America are purely elective—done on healthy women to end the lives of healthy children.[45]

When you cite these statistics, emphasize that they come from the abortion industry's own research group, the Guttmacher Institute, and avoid making editorial comments about the findings (e.g., "majority were for convenience"). It is compelling simply to say that the vast majority of abortions are "purely elective" abortions, done on healthy women with healthy babies.

Prepare for Common Pro-choice Arguments

One argument that often appears in discussions regarding abortion is this: "Outlawing abortion will mean back-alley butchers and countless women dying." Your rejoinder may include several points, but you should always start here: Overturning *Roe* doesn't make abortion illegal. It simply changes the venue of the question: from nine unelected Supreme Court justices to the people who can enact abortion policy through their elected state

---

45. Lawrence B. Finer et al., 113–14. This survey shows women have abortions for the following reasons: 25% "not ready for a(nother) child/ timing is wrong"; 23% "can't afford a baby now"; 19% "have completed my childbearing/have other people depending on me/children are grown"; 8% "don't want to be a single mother/am having relationship problems"; 7% "don't feel mature enough to raise a(nother) child/feel too young"; 6% "other" (this category had no further explanation); 4% "would interfere with education or career plans"; 4% "physical problem with my health"; 3% "possible problems affecting the health of the fetus"; -0.5% "husband or partner wants me to have an abortion"; -0.5%"parents want me to have an abortion"; -0.5% "don't want people to know I had sex or got pregnant"; -0.5% "was a victim of rape."

representatives.[46] Abortion is one of the most important issues of our day; it should be in the hands of the people.

You may want to concede the point that, even after limitations are established, there will always be people willing to break the law and exploit vulnerable women for financial gain. But because a destructive activity will not be completely eradicated is no reason to make or keep it legal (think of drug laws or laws against prostitution). No compassionate person wants a woman to suffer through the personal tragedy of abortion, whether legal or illegal. As Feminists for Life says, women deserve better than abortion. Establishing legal limits to the current "absolute right to abortion" will mean fewer abortions, and that is to the good of women, children, families, and society.

There are several points to make regarding the charge that countless women will die. First, it is impossible to calculate the number of maternal deaths from abortion before *Roe v. Wade* because they were not reported, so any claim regarding the number of maternal deaths from illegal abortions is purely speculative. However, abortion industry insider Bernard Nathanson admitted to circulating false numbers. Dr. Nathanson co-founded NARAL[47] and was director of the Center for Reproductive and Sexual Health in New York City, at one time the largest abortion clinic in the western world. In 1979 Nathanson said:

---

46. A federal law on the subject would be limited by the reach of the Commerce Clause according to the current view of the Supreme Court. Any effort to amend the Constitution would require passage by two-thirds of both houses of Congress and ratification by three-fifths of the states, no easy feat.
47. Originally called the National Alliance to Repeal Abortion Laws; today called NARAL Pro-Choice America

How many deaths were we talking about when abortion was illegal? In NARAL we generally emphasized the drama of the individual case, not the mass statistics, but when we spoke of the latter it was always "5,000–10,000 deaths a year." I confess that I knew the figures were totally false, and I suppose that others did too if they stopped to think of it. But in the "morality" of our revolution it was a useful figure, widely accepted, so why go out of our way to correct it with honest statistics? The overriding concern was to get the laws eliminated, and anything within reason that had to be done was permissible.[48]

Another abortion industry insider disputed the "back-alley butcher" notion in the decade before *Roe v. Wade*. In 1960, Dr. Mary Calderone, a former medical director for Planned Parenthood, estimated that nine out of ten illegal abortions were done by licensed doctors: "They are physicians, trained as such. … Abortion, whether therapeutic or illegal, is in the main no longer dangerous, because it is being done well by physicians."[49] We don't have to agree with Calderone that abortion is not dangerous to cite her statement that illegal abortions were done as well as legal ones. In fact, according to the Centers for Disease Control and Prevention, hundreds of women have died from abortion since *Roe v. Wade*.[50] This is likely only a fraction of the

---

48. Bernard Nathanson, *Aborting America* (New York: Doubleday & Co., 1979), 197.
49. Mary S. Calderone, "Illegal Abortion as Public Health Problem," American Journal of Public Health 50 (July 1960): 949, accessed January 21, 2011, http://ajph.aphapublications.org/cgi/re print/50/7/948.pdf.
50. The Centers for Disease Control and Prevention have received reports of the deaths of 439 women from induced abortion since Roe v. Wade; the latest year reported is 2006. Centers for Disease Control and Prevention, "Abortion

actual number in light of the fact that several states (including California) have failed to report abortion data for many years,[51] as well as the latitude given to doctors in reporting causes of death (e.g., "hemorrhage" rather than "induced abortion").[52]

Additionally, the experience of other countries shows that restricting abortion does not cause a rise in maternal deaths. Despite its tight abortion restrictions, Ireland has the lowest maternal mortality rate in the world, according to a study by

---

Surveillance—United States, 2007," *Morbidity and Mortality Weekly Report*, Surveillance Studies, 60, no. SS–01 (2011), accessed March 16, 2011, http://www.cdc.gov/mmwr/pre-view/mmwrhtml/ss6001a1.htm?s_cid=ss6001a1_w. See "Induced Termination of Pregnancy Before and After Roe v. Wade," *Journal of the American Medical Association*, 268 (Dec. 1992): 3231–3239.

51. Centers for Disease Control and Prevention, "Abortion Surveillance—United States, 2007," 3, 36.

52. Centers for Disease Control and Prevention, "Pregnancy-Related Mortality Surveillance—United States, 1991–1999," *Morbidity and Mortality Weekly Report*, Surveillance Studies 52, no. SS–02 (2003), accessed March 22, 2011, http://www.cdc.gov/mmwr/preview/mmwrhtml/ss5202a1.htm. This same report also found that "among women whose pregnancies ended in a spontaneous or induced abortion, infection was the cause of death for 34% of the women, followed by hemorrhage (22%) and other medical conditions (16%)." See also Isabelle L. Horon, "Underreporting of Maternal Deaths on Death Certificates and the Magnitude of the Problem of Maternal Mortality," *American Journal of Public Health* 95 (March 2005): 478–82 ("thirty-eight percent of maternal deaths were unreported on death certificates. Half or more deaths were unreported for women who were undelivered at the time of death, experienced a fetal death *or therapeutic abortion*, died more than a week after delivery, or died as a result of a cardiovascular disorder" [emphasis added]). In an investigation of state documents David Reardon et al. found that three abortion-related deaths occurred in 1989 in Maryland, though official Maryland statistics showed no abortion-related deaths for that year. See "Deaths Associated with Abortion Compared to Childbirth—a Review of New and Old Data and the Medical and Legal Implications," *Journal of Contemporary Health Law & Policy* 20 (2004): 279–327.

several agencies at the United Nations.[53] Malta also has substantial abortion limitations and one of the lowest maternal death-rates worldwide, lower than the United States.[54] Data compiled by Polish government agencies shows a marked decrease in maternal deaths once abortion was made illegal.[55]

Ultimately, the Supreme Court created a virtually unlimited right to abortion, a policy with which most Americans disagree. Our country is not divided down the middle on abortion—most of America is substantially with us. As we continue to expose the truth about abortion law and practice, we will move closer to the day that abortion policy-making is returned to the people.

Arguing from Women's Rights

The modern pro-choice movement is desperate to protect the image of abortion as positive and pro-woman. Ironically, their biggest threat is from those they claim to champion: women. Abortion-rights proponents are devastated by the women of the Silent No More Awareness Campaign, for example, who

---

53. The risk of death from maternal causes in Ireland is 1 in 100,000. See World Health Organization, "Maternal Mortality in 2005: Estimates Developed by WHO, UNFPA, and The World Bank," accessed April 4, 2011, http://www.who.int/whosis/mme_2005.pdf.

54. The risk of death from maternal causes in Malta is 8 in 100,000; in the United States it is 11 in 100,000. In Cuba, where abortion is highly liberalized and widely practiced, the rate of maternal death is 45 in 100,000. Ibid., 25–27.

55. In 1990 when abortion was legal in Poland, there were 70 maternal mortalities; in 2005, when abortion was illegal, maternal mortality related deaths were 24. See Center of Information Systems of Health Care, "Demographic Situation in Poland," Statistics Research Program of Public Statistics, 2001–2003; and Polish Central Statistical Office, "Demographic Yearbook,"1995–2003.

stand with their "I regret my abortion" signs.[56] They also face opposition from the powerful Feminists for Life, who argue that "women deserve better than abortion."[57]

Tell the Stories of Women

Pro-life men and women alike can point to the brave women coming forward in ever-greater numbers to speak out about how abortion was not an act of empowerment but the result of abandonment, betrayal, and desperation, and how it has negatively affected their lives. It is important to be accurate in your representation of these women.

The website After Abortion (http://afterabortion.org/), established by a woman who had five abortions, provides a place for women to help each other cope with the aftermath of their abortions. There are nearly 2.5 million posts. Women tell stories of how they were coerced into aborting their children by boyfriends, husbands, friends, and family. They describe how abortion was far from being a choice. They speak of overwhelming guilt, nightmares, excessive drinking, drug abuse, promiscuity, an inability to form or maintain relationships, difficulty bonding with later children, and other ways in which they are suffering. The stories on this site demonstrate the real impact of abortion on women.

Explain Why Being Pro-Life Is Being a True Feminist

Abortion advocates are also threatened by the pro-woman/pro-life arguments of the organization Feminists for Life, which

---

56. Referring to the Silent No More Awareness Campaign; see http://www.silentnomoreawareness.org.

57. "Feminists for Life Mission," Feminists for Life, accessed January 24, 2011, http://www.feministsfor-life.org/.

says abortion is a reflection that society has failed to meet the needs of women.[58] Pro-woman/pro-life arguments are destroying the old "baby vs. woman" dichotomy that has dominated the abortion debate for decades. Women and children are not natural enemies; it was a perversion of feminism that brought about such a dichotomy in the first place. Visit the Feminists for Life website to read their pro-life answers to "pro-choice" questions, and commit them to memory.

Roe-era feminists like Kate Michelman, the former president of NARAL Pro-Choice America, proclaimed abortion to be "the guarantor of a woman's right to participate fully in the social and political life of society."[59] But pro-life feminists believe this idea turns feminism on its head because it says women don't have an inherent right to participate in society but one conditioned on surgery and sacrificing their children. No women should have to abort her child to participate fully in society. The true feminist response holds that if a pregnant woman or mother can't participate in society, something is wrong with society.

Michelman's statement is also at odds with the views of America's first feminists, all of whom opposed abortion. Chief among them were Susan B. Anthony and Elizabeth Cady Stanton, who not only led the fight for the right of women to own property, to vote, and to obtain equal education, but also spoke out against abortion. Susan B. Anthony's newspaper, *The Revolution*, called abortion "child murder" and "infanticide."[60] In 1869 Anthony said, "No matter what the motive, love of

---

58. Ibid.

59. Tamar Lewin, "Legal Abortion Under Fierce Attack 15 Years After Roe v. Wade Ruling," *New York Times*, May 10, 1988, accessed March 15, 2011 http://www.nytimes.com/1988/05/10/us/legal-abortion-under-fierce-attack-15-years-after-roe-v-wade-ruling.html?scp=2&sq=&pagewanted=all.

60. *The Revolution*, April 9, 1868 . See also *The Revolution*, July 8, 1869.

ease, or a desire to save from suffering the unborn innocent, the woman is awfully guilty who commits the deed. It will burden her conscience in life, it will burden her soul in death; But oh, thrice guilty is he who drove her to the desperation which impelled her to the crime!"[61]

Ultimately, the efforts of modern pro-life feminists are destroying the old "baby vs. woman" dichotomy that dominated the abortion debate for decades. They are recasting the other side in their true light: not as defenders of women but as defenders of abortion. To be pro-life is to embrace the tenets of non-violence and equal justice for all—the true tenets of feminism heralded by America's first feminists.

Conclusion

The more a person understands abortion, the more he or she realizes it is anti-human, anti-life, and anti-woman. The notion that we are in the business of "changing hearts and minds" has, regrettably, been reduced to cliché, but it is nevertheless true. Abortion is different from any other modern social issue debated today, and many people are suffering because of it. Prayerfully, and for the sake of women and their babies, let us go after those hearts and minds armed with knowledge and animated by compassion.

---

61. Susan B. Anthony, *The Revolution*, July 8, 1869.

NEED HELP NOW

Option Line

www.optionline.org

If you are wondering whether you're pregnant, your mind is probably racing with questions. It's common to feel confused, scared, or overwhelmed. Option Line live chat is available any time, day or night. You can call 800-712-HELP or text HELPLINE to 313131.

Option Line offers free, confidential help, information about pregnancy signs and symptoms, and information on all your options. They can quickly connect you to the local assistance you need.

Their helpful website will give you links to all the pregnancy centers across America. If you have questions about pregnancy, the morning-after pill, abortion, or even battling post abortion symptoms, contact Option Line today.

For an additional list of nearby pregnancy centers, visit www.prolifeunity.com.

SUPPORT

I Am Pro-Life

www.facebook.com/focusonlife

Join more than 900,000 people who have taken a stand for life. Learn more about the pro-life movement and share words of encouragement, hope, and bold declaration in defense of the defenseless.

RECOMMENDED MINISTRIES

Choose Life America, Inc.

www.choose-life.org

Choose Life, Inc. was formed in Florida in 1996 with the idea to use license plate sales to help fund efforts for pre-natal care for women considering adoption services. They also help pro-life pregnancy centers and other life affirming agencies get services to women who need them.

Christian Legal Society

www.clsnet.org

The Christian Legal Society's mission is to "inspire, encourage, and equip lawyers and law students, both individually and in community, to proclaim, love, and serve Jesus Christ through the study and practice of law, the provision of legal assistance to the poor, and the defense of religious freedom and [the] sanctity of human life." As a national grassroots network, the society also advocates biblical conflict resolution and public justice.

Dr. James Dobson's Family Talk

www.drjamesdobson.org

Family Talk is a national ministry with a mission to help preserve and promote the institution of the family and the biblical principles on which it is based, and to seek to introduce as many people as possible to the gospel of Jesus Christ. Specifically, the focus of the ministry is on marriage, parenthood, evangelism, the sanctity of human life, and encouraging righteousness in the culture.

Family Research Council

www.frc.org

Founded in 1983, Family Research Council (FRC) is a nonprofit research and educational organization dedicated to articulating and advancing a family-centered philosophy of public life. In addition to providing policy research and analysis for the legislative, executive, and judicial branches of the federal government, FRC seeks to inform the news media, the academic community, business leaders, and the general public about family issues that affect the nation.

Focus on the Family

www.focusonthefamily.com

Focus on the Family is a global Christian ministry dedicated to helping families thrive. They provide help and resources for couples to build healthy marriages that reflect God's design, and for parents to raise their children according to morals and values grounded in biblical principles. For information on

Option Ultrasound and Sanctity of Human Life projects and newsletters, visit www.heartlink.org.

LifeNews

www.lifenews.com

Formerly the Pro-Life Infonet, LifeNews.com has been harnessing the power of the Internet since 1992 to bring pro-life news to the pro-life community. With a team of experienced journalists and bloggers, LifeNews.com reaches more than 750,000 pro-life advocates each week via their website, email news reports, social networking outreach, and weekday radio program.

National Day of Prayer

www.NationalDayofPrayer.org

The National Day of Prayer is an annual observance held on the first Thursday of May, inviting people of all faiths to pray for the nation. It was created in 1952 by a joint resolution of the United States Congress and signed into law by President Harry S. Truman. More than 40,000 Christian events are organized annually across the country by the National Day of Prayer Task Force, led by Mrs. Shirley Dobson and Mr. John Bornschein.

National Right to Life

www.nrlc.org

The National Right to Life organization is the largest, nationwide network of pro-life people dedicated entirely to protecting life.

Pro-life Action League

www.prolifeaction.org

The Pro-Life Action League was founded by Joseph M. Scheidler in 1980 with the aim of saving unborn children through non-violent direct action. The League is a national organization dedicated to empowering Americans to put their pro-life convictions into effective action in their local communities.

RECOMMENDED RESOURCES

For your continued education and understanding of the physical, spiritual, and psychological effects abortion is having on individuals, families, and societies, I highly encourage you to consider the following resources.

Alcorn, Randy. *ProLife Answers to ProChoice Arguments.* Sisters, Oreg.: Multnomah, 2000.

———. *Why ProLife? Caring for the Unborn and Their Mothers.* Sisters, Oreg.: Multnomah, 2004.

Becker, Daniel C. *Personhood: A Pragmatic Guide to Prolife Victory in the 21st Century and the Return to First Principles in Politics.* Alpharetta, Ga.: TKS Publications, 2011.

Klusendorf, Scott. *The Case for Life: Equipping Christians to Engage the Culture.* Wheaton, Ill.: Crossway Books and Bibles, 2009.

ABOUT THE AUTHORS

John Bornschein

John is the vice-chariman of the National Day of Prayer Task Force and an executive member of the National Prayer Committee. During his 18 years in ministry, John has engaged in a vast range of responsibilities, including serving as a missionary and senior pastor, as well as with Mission of Mercy (One Child Matters), Heritage Builders, and Focus on the Family.

John is the executive producer of "Drive Thru History: America," the video curriculum in the popular series seen on History Channel International and Trinity Broadcasting Network. As an executive producer, John has also worked alongside some of the best creative minds in Nashville, turning out powerful patriotic and worshipful songs such as "Let Freedom Ring" by Dennis Jernigan (Doxology Records), "America" with Rebecca St. James (ForeFront Records), and "We Pray" with BarlowGirl (Fervent).

As an author, John has contributed to dozens of resources, including the books *Heal Our Land, Compassion Revolution, Start Your Family, Together in Prayer* and *Celebration Parenthood* (forthcoming). He recently completed a new book for the National Day of Prayer titled, *The Front Line: A Prayer Warrior's*

Guide to Spiritual Battle. In addition, he has written for several publications including *Horizon, Prayer Lines,* and *Focus on the Family* magazine.

John is a frequent guest on radio programs across the nation and has hosted the Focus on the Family broadcast and Life Today on Salem networks. He is currently a co-host of the Pray for America podcast.

John serves as the senior pastor at Calvary Fellowship Fountain Valley church, holds a B.Th, and is currently pursuing a Master of Divinity degree from Bethany Baptist Seminary. John is also a speaker at the popular *Spiritual Growth of Children* Conferences, attended by thousands around the country.

He has served at the United Nations in New York and with our congressional leaders in Washington D.C., as a representative for the National Day of Prayer. But his true joy is his wife, Brandi, and their five children who love the Lord. They reside in Colorado Springs, Colorado.

Cathy Cleaver Ruse

Cathy Cleaver Ruse is senior fellow for legal studies at Family Research Council. Previously, she served as chief counsel for the U.S. House of Representatives Constitution Subcommittee and was the pro-life spokesperson for the U.S. Conference of Catholic Bishops. She received a law degree from Georgetown University.

Rob Schwarzwalder

Rob Schwarzwalder is senior vice president of Family Research Council. He formerly served as a presidential appointee at the U.S. Department of Health and Human Services, where as senior speech writer he crafted language on all facets of federal health care policy. Previously, he was chief of staff to two members of Congress.

Spiritual Warfare Is Here—
Are You Ready to Fight Back?

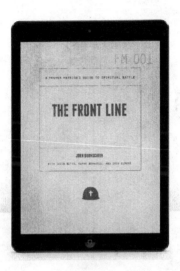

It's a critical hour. The church is in need of an awakening, and our nation is desperate for spiritual revival. *The Front Line* is your field guide for using our most powerful God-given tool for real-world change: prayer. Equip yourself for spiritual warfare—start training to be a prayer warrior today.

Download the free Vyrso app—the best in Christian mobile reading—and get *The Front Line* for 25% off the retail price.

Visit Vyrso.com/FrontLine to learn more.

Vyrso.com • 888-875-9491 • +1 360-685-4437 (Int'l)